FOR PEOPLE *who* LOVE BOOKS

Much —
Read + write
Be Happy

# For People Who Love Books

*Over 2,000 Mind Activating Thoughts*

*A Companion for Writers, Authors, Editors, Agents,*
*Publishers, Librarians,*
*Book Sellers, Readers*
*and Book Lovers*

## ARTHUR Q. GUTCH

ISBN 0-7414-5800-4

Printed in the United States of America

Published January 2010

INFINITY PUBLISHING
1094 New DeHaven Street, Suite 100
West Conshohocken, PA 19428-2713
Toll-free (877) BUY BOOK
Local Phone (610) 941-9999
Fax (610) 941-9959
Info@buybooksontheweb.com
www.buybooksontheweb.com

*To the people who create, distribute and care for books and who serve us, so that we may experience the pleasures that books provide.*

*And*
*Lisa, Samantha and Olive who have supported my energetic love of books over the years.*

# Contents

A room without books is like a body
without a soul.
~ *Marcus Tullius Cicero*

# Personal Note to Reader

Books have always been a special part of my life. Browsing amongst the bookshelves, flipping through the pages (paper or digital), absorbing the knowledge, making an acquisition and *then* reading my discoveries have given me countless hours of enjoyment. The impetus for this compilation came out of my own quest to write a book. Having found it very difficult to stay inspired and motivated I concluded there must be thousands of others who need some help to get the proverbial juices flowing.

This book is perfect for the seasoned or novice author, bookstore owner, librarian, publisher, editor or active reader. In presenting this compilation of thought-provoking insights related to books, it is my hope that you will harvest the messages and wisdom of those speaking from the page to, in some way, better your work and life. It is a great companion for those who participate in the creation and delivery of books, who want a recent or ancient perspective that will inspire you to clarify your purpose and achieve your potential.

*The New Book*
Over three billion books were purchased domestically in 2008 evidence that we are not alone and that people still love books. In fact, in 2008 over 500,000 new book titles were introduced in the United States. While the number of books absorbed by readers is growing, the subject matter is expanding into previously unrepresented niche categories. This is being driven by the

efficiency of print-on-demand (POD) solutions that now allow authors and publishers to print one (1) book at a time, negating the need to sell a minimum number of books to cover the costs associated with the printing, warehousing and shipping of thousands of books that may never be sold. E-books, although only a small percentage of the current book market provide even greater efficiencies, where the cost to produce and distribute digital content is minimal. Electronic reading devices, once very expensive and unwieldy to hold have finally emerged to accommodate audio and e-book formats at a reasonable price. Online distribution offers a multitude of virtual bookstores from which to feed your interests. A new mixed media offering including print, e-books, and audio represent the new book with video and other innovations not too far behind.

*Author Originated Works*
For authors the publishing landscape is changing dramatically, and for the better. If you are thinking of offering your own masterpiece to the masses you can submit a finished manuscript and, within days or weeks, have it available on any number of online bookstores such as Amazon or Barnes & Noble for the global public to browse and buy. The old paradigm whereby submitting a manuscript resulted in rejection letters for 99% of authors is changing. Authors now have publishing alternatives that can meet many of their needs if a "traditional publisher" decides not to purchase their work. The new online paradigm which includes marketplaces like Amazon and a myriad of methods to promote your book by virtually writing your way to success has changed publishing forever. In the end, the more relevant you can be to your audience the more successful you will be.

*Being Relevant Matters*

For readers the sheer number and variety of books is increasing rapidly. A book that may interest the smallest population of readers can now be efficiently created, offered and purchased online. A new global wave of knowledge is coming. In the future the reader and author will have more control, as tools for book creation, distribution and content filtering make it easier to deliver and find relevant subject matter wherever you may be.

Did you ever think you could begin reading a great novel in the evening in front of the fireplace, in the morning listen to it on the ride to work, and then, while at the beach on the weekend pull out your digital reader to finish the job?

*What an amazing time for people who love books!*

# How to Use This Book

Read for pure enjoyment and think of this book as your companion when you are looking for new ideas and solutions to challenges you may encounter in work and life. The thoughts in this book are especially relevant to those involved in the creation, distribution and care of books.

The relevant connections between the thoughts in this book and the millions already in your consciousness are infinite. How you use these connections to generate your own flashes of brilliance is up to you. Any time you have a question that is looking for an answer pick up the book and reflect on the insights and wisdom from recent and ancient times.

∞ When you have a new challenge and are looking for insights in order to develop a unique solution

∞ When you are looking for a truly new idea and need some fresh perspectives in the context of books

∞ When you need a little motivation or flash of brilliance to complete that next chapter

∞ When you need to get into the minds of authors, readers or the people that love books

∞ When the words are just not there, and you need some inspiration from writers who came before you.

*Let the thoughts flow...!*

FOR PEOPLE *who* LOVE BOOKS

# On Books

Show me the books he loves and I shall know the man far better than through mortal friends.
~ *Dawn Adams*

Books are men of higher stature; the only men that speak aloud for future times to hear.
~ *E.S. Barrett*

A house is not a home unless it contains food and fire for the mind as well as the body.
~ *Margaret Fuller*

Outside of a dog, a book is a man's best friend. Inside of a dog, it's too dark to read.
~ *Groucho Marx*

Books are not men and yet they stay alive.
~ *Stephen Vincent Benet*

The world may be full of fourth-rate writers but it's also full of fourth-rate readers.
~ *Stan Barstow*

A book is a garden, an orchard, a storehouse, a party, a company by the way, a counselor, a multitude of counselors.
~ *Henry Ward Beecher*

All the best stories in the world are but one story in reality ~ the story of escape. It is the only thing which interests us all and at all times, how to escape.
~ *Arthur Christopher Benson*

I read the newspaper avidly. It is my one form of continuous fiction.
~ *Aneurin Bevan*

A conventional good read is usually a bad read, a relaxing bath in what we know already. A true good read is surely an act of innovative creation in which we, the readers, become conspirators.
~ *Malcolm Bradbury*

You don't have to burn books to destroy a culture. Just get people to stop reading them.
~ *Ray Bradbury*

It is well to read everything of something, and something of everything.
~ *Lord Henry P. Brougham*

Books, books, books had found the secret of a garret-room piled high with cases in my father's name; Piled high, packed large, where, creeping in and out among the giant fossils of my past,

like some small nimble mouse between the ribs of a mastodon, I nibbled here and there at this or that box, pulling through the gap, in heats of terror, haste, victorious joy, the first book first. And how I felt it beat under my pillow, in the morning's dark. An hour before the sun would let me read! My books!
~ *Elizabeth Barrett Browning*

Books are masters who instruct us without rods or ferules, without words or anger, without bread or money. If you approach them, they are not asleep; if you seek them, they do not hide; if you blunder, they do not scold; if you are ignorant, they do not laugh at you.
~ *Richard De Bury*

Surviving and thriving as a professional today demands two new approaches to the written word. First, it requires a new approach to orchestrating information, by skillfully choosing what to read and what to ignore. Second, it requires a new approach to integrating information, by reading faster and with greater comprehension.
~ *Jimmy Calano*

A novel is never anything, but a philosophy put into images.
~ *Albert Camus*

After all manner of professors have done their best for us, the place we are to get knowledge is in books. The true university of these days is a collection of books.
~ *Thomas Carlyle*

The novel can't compete with cars, the movies, television, and liquor. A guy who's had a good feed and tanked up on good wine gives his old lady a kiss after supper and his day is over. Finished.
~ *Louis-Ferdinand Celine*

Books are standing counselors and preachers, always at hand, and always disinterested; having this advantage over oral instructors, that they are ready to repeat their lesson as often as we please.
~ *Oswald Chambers*

Books are the blessed chloroform of the mind.
~ *Robert Chambers*

A good title is the title of a successful book.
~ *Raymond Chandler*

The flood of print has turned reading into a process of gulping rather than savoring
~ *Warren Chappell*

Let blockheads read what blockheads wrote.
~ *Lord Chesterfield*

The mere brute pleasure of reading ~ the sort of pleasure a cow must have in grazing.
~ *Gilbert K. Chesterton*

Books are but waste paper unless we spend in action the wisdom we get from thought ~ asleep. When we are weary of the living, we may repair to the dead, who have nothing of peevishness, pride, or design in their conversation.
~ *Jeremy Collier*

A room without books is like a body without a soul.
~ *Marcus Tullius Cicero*

Perhaps there are none more lazy, or more truly ignorant, than your everlasting readers.
~ *William Cobbett*

You are wise, witty and wonderful, but you spend too much time reading this sort of stuff.
~ *Jim Critchfield*

The great American novel has not only already been written, it has already been rejected.
~ *Frank Dane*

Next, in importance to books are their titles.
~ *Paul Davies*

If I had my way books would not be written in English, but in an exceedingly difficult secret language that only skilled professional readers and story-tellers could interpret. Then people like you would have to go to public halls and pay good prices to hear the professionals decode and read the books aloud for you. This plan would have the advantage of scaring off all amateur authors, retired politicians, country doctors and I-Married-a-Midget writers who would not have the patience to learn the secret language.
~ *Robertson Davies*

The man who is fond of books is usually a man of lofty thought, and of elevated opinions.
~ *Christopher Dawson*

The world of books is the most remarkable creation of man nothing else that he builds ever lasts monuments fall; nations perish; civilization grow old and die out; new races build others. But in the world of books are volumes that have seen this happen again and again and yet live on. Still young, still as fresh as the day they were written, still telling men's hearts, of the hearts of men centuries dead.
~ *Clarence Day*

He that loves a book will never want a faithful friend, a wholesome counselor, a cheerful companion, an effectual comforter. By study, by reading, by thinking, one may innocently divert and pleasantly entertain himself, as in all weathers, as in all fortunes.
~ *John Barrow*

There is an art of reading, as well as an art of thinking, and an art of writing.
~ *Isaac Disraeli*

Never judge a book by its movie.
~ *J. W. Eagan*

Readers are less and less seen as mere non-writers, the subhuman other or flawed derivative of the author; the lack of a pen is no longer a shameful mark of secondary status but a positively enabling space, just as within every writer can be seen to lurk, as a repressed but contaminating antithesis, a reader.
~ *Terry Eagleton*

The successful Accelerated Reader is able to read larger than normal blocks or bites of the printed page with each eye stop. He has accepted, without reservation, the philosophy that the most important benefit of reading is the gaining of information, ideas, mental picture and entertainment-not the fretting over words. He has come to the realization that words in and of themselves are for the most part insignificant.

~ *Wade E. Cutler*

Our high respect for a well read person is praise enough for literature.

~ *Ralph Waldo Emerson*

There is a set of religious, or rather moral, writings which teach that virtue is the certain road to happiness, and vice to misery in this world. A very wholesome and comfortable doctrine, and to which we have but one objection, namely, that it is not true.

~ *Henry Fielding*

Read much, but not many books.

~ *Benjamin Franklin*

When you have mastered numbers, you will in fact no longer be reading numbers, any more than you read words when reading books You will be reading meanings.

~ *Harold S. Geneen*

I know every book of mine by its smell, and I have but to put my nose between the pages to be reminded of all sorts of things.

~ *George Robert Gissing*

I have read your book and much like it.

~ *Moses Hadas*

The first time I read an excellent work, it is to me just as if I gained a new friend; and when I read over a book I have perused before, it resembles the meeting of an old one.
~ *Sir James Goldsmith*

A book might be written on the injustice of the just.
~ *Anthony Hope*

Books give not wisdom where none was before. But where some is, there reading makes it more.
~ *John Harington*

The best of a book is not the thought which it contains, but the thought which it suggests; just as the charm of music dwells not in the tones but in the echoes of our hearts.
~ *Oliver Wendell Holmes*

The books we read should be chosen with great care, that they may be, as an Egyptian king wrote over his library, the medicines of the soul.
~ *Paxton Hood*

The newest books are those that never grow old.
~ *George Holbrook Jackson*

Read as you taste fruit or savor wine, or enjoy friendship, love or life.
~ *Holbrook Jackson*

Books constitute capital. A library book lasts as long as a house, for hundreds of years. It is not, then, an article of mere consumption but fairly of capital, and often in the case of professional men, setting out in life, it is their only capital.
~ *Thomas Jefferson*

Tradition is but a meteor, which, if it once falls, cannot be rekindled. Memory, once interrupted, is not to be recalled. But written learning is a fixed luminary, which, after the cloud that had hidden it has passed away, is again bright in its proper station. So books are faithful repositories, which may be awhile neglected or forgotten, but when opened again, will again impart instruction.

~ *Samuel Johnson*

Books that you carry to the fire, and hold readily in your hand, are most useful after all.

~ *Samuel Johnson*

The worst thing about new books is that they keep us from reading the old ones.

~ *Joseph Joubert*

The Bible remained for me a book of books, still divine ~ but divine in the sense that all great books are divine which teach men how to live righteously.

~ *Sir Arthur Keith*

Everywhere I have sought rest and not found it, except sitting in a corner by myself with a little book.

~ *Thomas ã Kempis*

I am a part of everything that I have read.

~ *John Kieran*

Borrowers of books ~ those mutilators of collections, spoilers of the symmetry of shelves, and creators of odd volumes.

~ *Charles Lamb*

Until I feared I would lose it, I never loved to read. One does not love breathing.
~ *Harper Lee*

A bad book is the worse that it cannot repent. It has not been the devil's policy to keep the masses of mankind in ignorance; but finding that they will read, he is doing all in his power to poison their books.
~ *E.N. Kirk*

You can either read something many times in order to be assured that you got it all, or else you can define your purpose and use techniques which will assure that you have met it and gotten what you need.
~ *Peter Kump*

The printing press is either the greatest blessing or the greatest curse of modern times, sometimes one forgets which it is.
~ *Sir James M. Barrie*

After all, the world is not a stage ~ not to me: nor a theatre: nor a show-house of any sort. And art, especially novels, are not little theatres where the reader sits aloft and watches... and sighs, commiserates, condones and smiles. That's what you want a book to be: because it leaves you so safe and superior, with your two-dollar ticket to the show. And that's what my books are not and never will be. Whoever reads me will be in the thick of the scrimmage, and if he doesn't like it ~ if he wants a safe seat in the audience ~ let him read someone else.
~ *D. H. Lawrence*

You've really got to start hitting the books because it's no joke out here.
~ *Spike Lee*

For a good book has this quality, that it is not merely a petrifaction of its author, but that once it has been tossed behind, like Deucalion's little stone, it acquires a separate and vivid life of its own.
~ *Caroline Lejeune*

I feel like I'm drowning. Every night, I'm carrying home loads of things to read but I'm too exhausted. I keep clipping things and Xeroxing them and planning to read them eventually, but I just end up throwing it all away and feeling guilty.
~ *Ghita Levine*

A book is a mirror: If an ass peers into it, you can't expect an apostle to look out.
~ *Georg C. Lichtenberg*

For books are more than books, they are the life, the very heart and core of ages past, the reason why men lived and worked and died, the essence and quintessence of their lives.
~ *Amy Lowell*

In science, read by preference the newest works. In literature, read the oldest. The classics are always modern.
~ *Lord Edward Lytton*

A novel must be exceptionally good to live as long as the average cat.
~ *Hugh Maclennan*

Any book that helps a child to form a habit of reading, to make reading one of his deep and continuing needs, is good for him.
~ *Richard McKenna*

Everything in the world exists to end up in a book.
~ *Stephane Mallarme*

Readers are plentiful: thinkers are rare.
~ *Harriet Martineau*

The book to read is not the one which thinks for you, but the one which makes you think. No book in the world equals the Bible for that.
~ *Mccosh*

A dose of poison can do its work but once. A bad book can go on poisoning minds for generations.
~ *William Murray*

There are people who read too much: bibliobibuli. I know some who are constantly drunk on books, as other men are drunk on whiskey or religion. They wander through this most diverting and stimulating of worlds in a haze, seeing nothing and hearing nothing.
~ *H. L. Mencken*

Until it is kindled by a spirit as flamingly alive as the one which gave it birth a book is dead to us. Words divested of their magic are but dead hieroglyphs.
~ *Henry Miller*

Deep versed in books and shallow in himself.
~ *John Milton*

Books and marriage go ill together.
~ *Molière (Jean-Baptiste Poquelin)*

Some of the most famous books are the least worth reading. Their fame was due to their having done something that needed to be doing in their day. The work is done and the virtue of the book has expired.
~ *John Morely*

A bibliophile of little means is likely to suffer often. Books don't slip from his hands but fly past him through the air, high as birds, high as prices.
~ *Pablo Neruda*

The books that help you most are those which make you think that most. The hardest way of learning is that of easy reading; but a great book that comes from a great thinker is a ship of thought, deep freighted with truth and beauty.
~ *Theodore Parker*

The last thing one discovers in composing a work is what to put first.
~ *Blaise Pascal*

The more sins you confess, the more books you will sell.
~ *American Proverb*

This book fills a much-needed gap.
~ *Moses Hadas*

She could give herself up to the written word as naturally as a good dancer to music or a fine swimmer to water. The only difficulty was that after finishing the last sentence she was left

with a feeling at once hollow and uncomfortably full. Exactly like indigestion.
~ *Jean Rhys*

Reading makes immigrants of us all. It takes us away from home, but more important, it finds homes for us everywhere.
~ *Hazel Rochman*

Upon books the collective education of the race depends; they are the sole instruments of registering, perpetuating and transmitting thought.
~ *Henry C. Rogers*

The reason that fiction is more interesting than any other form of literature, to those who really like to study people, is that in fiction the author can really tell the truth without humiliating himself.
~ *Eleanor Roosevelt*

Very young children eat their books, literally devouring their contents. This is one reason for the scarcity of first editions of Alice in Wonderland and other favorites of the nursery.
~ *A. S. W. Rosenbach*

The real risks for any artist are taken in pushing the work to the limits of what is possible, in the attempt to increase the sum of what it is possible to think. Books become good when they go to this edge and risk falling over it ~ when they endanger the artist by reason of what he has, or has not, artistically dared.
~ *Salman Rushdie*

Books are like a mirror. If an ass looks in, you can't expect an angel to look out.
~ *Arthur Schopenhauer*

Prerequisite for re-readability in books: that they be forgettable.
~ *Jean Rostand*

To use books rightly, is to go to them for help; to appeal to them when our own knowledge and power fail; to be led by them into wider sight and purer conception than our own, and to receive from them the united sentence of the judges and councils of all time, against our solitary and unstable opinions.
~ *John Ruskin*

I've never know any trouble than an hour's reading didn't assuage.
~ *Charles de Secondat*

What is the most precious, the most exciting smell awaiting you in the house when you return to it after a dozen years or so? The smell of roses, you think? No, moldering books.
~ *Andre Sinyavsky*

A great book should leave you with many experiences and slightly exhausted at the end. You should live several lives while reading it.
~ *William Styron*

Most books, like their authors, are born to die; of only a few books can it be said that death has no dominion over them; they live, and their influence lives forever.
~ *J. Swartz*

People say that life is the thing, but I prefer reading.
~ *Logan Pearsall Smith*

Why pay a dollar for a bookmark? Why not use the dollar for a bookmark?
~ *Fred Stoller*

Books, like proverbs, receive their chief value from the stamp and esteem of the ages through which they have passed.
~ *Sir William Temple*

What is a diary as a rule? A document useful to the person who keeps it. Dull to the contemporary who reads it and invaluable to the student, centuries afterwards, who treasures it.
~ *Helen Terry*

Books, not which afford us a cowering enjoyment, but in which each thought is of unusual daring; such as an idle man cannot read, and a timid one would not be entertained by, which even make us dangerous to existing institution ~ such call I good books.
~ *Henry David Thoreau*

Read the best books first, or you may not have a chance to read them at all.
~ *Henry David Thoreau*

No matter how busy you may think you are, you must find time for reading, or surrender yourself to self-chosen ignorance.
~ *Atwood H. Townsend*

The Brahmins say that in their books there are many predictions of times in which it will rain. But press those books as strongly as you can, you can not get out of them a drop of water. So you can not get out of all the books that contain the best precepts the smallest good deed.
~ *Leo Tolstoy*

One half who graduate from college never read another book.
~ *Herbert True*

There are books so alive that you're always afraid that while you weren't reading, the book has gone and changed, has shifted like a river; while you went on living, it went on living too, and like a river moved on and moved away. No one has stepped twice into the same river. But did anyone ever step twice into the same book?
~ *Marina Tsvetaeva*

My books are water; those of the great geniuses are wine ~ everybody drinks water.
~ *Mark Twain*

Ideally a book would have no order to it, and the reader would have to discover his own.
~ *Raoul Vaneigem*

Fiction reveals truth that reality obscures.
~ *Jessamyn West*

Camerado! This is no book; who touches this touches a man.
~ *Walt Whitman*

Books had instant replay long before televised sports.
~ *Bert Williams*

Old books that have ceased to be of service should no more be abandoned than should old friends who have ceased to give pleasure.
~ *Sir Peregrine Worsthorne*

Choose an author as you choose a friend.
~ *Sir Christopher Wren*

Man ceased to be an ape, vanquished the ape, on the day the first book was written.
~ *Yevgeny Zamyatin*

Books are the legacies that a great genius leaves to mankind, which are delivered down from generation to generation as presents to the posterity of those who are yet unborn.
~ *Joseph Addison 1672-1719, British Essayist, Poet, Statesman*

In the case of good books, the point is not how many of them you can get through, but rather how many can get through to you.
~ *Mortimer J. Adler 1902-, American Educator, Philosopher*

That is a good book which is opened with expectation, and closed with delight and profit.
~ *Amos Bronson Alcott*

Beware of the person of one book.
~ *St. Thomas Aquinas 1225-1274, Italian Scholastic Philosopher*

A real book is not one that we read, but one that reads us.
~ *W. H. Auden, Anglo-American Poet 1907-1973*

Some books are undeservedly forgotten; none are undeservedly remembered.
~ *W. H. Auden, Anglo-American Poet 1907-1973*

Everything in this book may be wrong. [The Savior's Manual]
~ *Richard Bach, American Author 1936-*

Read not to contradict and confute; nor to believe and take for granted; nor to find talk and discourse; but to weigh and consider.
~ *Sir Francis Bacon 1561-1626, British Philosopher, Essayist*

Footnotes are the finer-suckered surfaces that allow testicular paragraphs to hold fast to the wider reality of the library.
~ *Nicholson Baker 1957-, American Author*

When the book comes out it may hurt you ~ but in order for me to do it, it had to hurt me first. I can only tell you about yourself as much as I can face about myself.
~ *James Baldwin 1924-1987, American Author*

Books are not made for furniture, but there is nothing else that so beautifully furnishes a house.
~ *Henry Ward Beecher*

When I am dead, I hope it may be said: "His sins were scarlet, but his books were read."
~ *Hilaire Belloc*

Of all the ways of acquiring books, writing them oneself is regarded as the most praiseworthy method. Writers are really people who write books not because they are poor, but because they are dissatisfied with the books which they could buy but do not like.
~ *Walter Benjamin, 1982-1940, German Critic, Philosopher*

Does there, I wonder, exist a being who has read all, or approximately all, that the person of average culture is supposed to have read, and that not to have read is a social sin? If such a being does exist, surely he is an old, a very old man.
~ *Arnold Bennett 1867-1931, British Novelist*

When we read a story, we inhabit it. The covers of the book are like a roof and four walls. What is to happen next will take place within the four walls of the story. And this is possible because the story's voice makes everything its own.
~ *John Berger 1926-, British Actor, Critic*

Read nothing that you do not care to remember, and remember nothing you do not mean to use.
~ *Professor Blackie*

The failure to read good books both enfeebles the vision and strengthens our most fatal tendency ~ the belief that the here and now is all there is.
~ *Allan Bloom 1930-1992, American Educator, Author*

There are worse crimes than burning books. One of them is not reading them.
~ *Joseph Brodsky 1940-, Russian-born American Poet, Critic*

A book may be compared to your neighbor: if it be good, it cannot last too long; if bad, you cannot get rid of it too early.
~ *Rupert Brooke 1887-1915, British Poet*

The lessons taught in great books are misleading. The commerce in life is rarely so simple and never so just.
~ *Anita Brookner 1938-, British Novelist, Art Historian*

Begin to read a book that will help you move toward your dream.
~ *Les Brown 1945-, American Speaker, Author, Trainer, Motivator Lecturer*

Books succeed, and lives fail.
~ *Elizabeth Barrett Browning 1806-1861, British Poet*

When a book raises your spirit, and inspires you with noble and manly thoughts, seek for no other test of its excellence. It is good, and made by a good workman.
~ *Jean De La Bruyère 1645-1696, French Classical Writer*

Read Homer once, and you can read no more. For all books else appear so mean, and so poor. Verse will seem prose; but still persist to read, and Homer will be all the books you need.
~ *Duke of Buckingham 1628-1687, Poet, Satirist, Dramatist*

In science read the newest works, in literature read the oldest.
~ *Edward G. Bulwer-Lytton 1803-1873, British Novelist, Poet*

Reading without purpose is sauntering not exercise.
~ *Edward G. Bulwer-Lytton 1803-1873, British Novelist, Poet*

Americans will listen, but they do not care to read. War and Peace must wait for the leisure of retirement, which never really comes: meanwhile it helps to furnish the living room. Blockbusting fiction is bought as furniture. Unread, it maintains its value. Read, it looks like money wasted. Cunningly, Americans know that books contain a person, and they want the person, not the book.
~ *Anthony Burgess 1917-1993, British Writer, Critic*

The oldest books are still only just out to those who have not read them.
~ *Samuel Butler 1612-1680, British Poet, Satirist*

The reading or non-reading a book will never keep down a single petticoat.
~ *Lord Byron 1788-1824, British Poet*

Tis pleasant, sure, to see one's name in print; A book's a book, although there's nothing in it.
~ *Lord Byron 1788-1824, British Poet*

A novel points out that the world consists entirely of exceptions.
~ *Joyce Carey*

If a book comes from the heart it will contrive to reach other hearts. All art and author craft are of small account to that.
~ *Thomas Carlyle 1795-1881, Scottish Philosopher, Author*

The best effect of any book, is that it excites the reader to self-activity.
~ *Thomas Carlyle 1795-1881, Scottish Philosopher, Author*

What we become depends on what we read after all the professors have finished with us. The greatest university of all is the collection of books.
~ *Thomas Carlyle 1795-1881, Scottish Philosopher, Author*

Reading a book is like re-writing it for yourself. You bring to a novel, anything you read, all your experience of the world. You bring your history and you read it in your own terms.
~ *Angela Carter 1940-1992, British Author*

A good book, in the language of the book-sellers, is a salable one; in that of the curious, a scarce one; in that of men of sense, a useful and instructive one.
~ *Oswald Chambers 1874-1917 Scottish Preacher, Author*

Most books today seemed to have been written overnight from books read the day before.
~ *Sebastien-Roch Nicolas De Chamfort 1741-1794, French Writer*

At least half the mystery novels published violate the law that the solution, once revealed, must seem to be inevitable.
~ *Raymond Chandler 1888-1959, American Author*

Every man is a volume if you know how to read him.
~ *William Ellery Channing 1780-1842, American Unitarian Minister*

It is chiefly through books that we enjoy intercourse with superior minds, and these invaluable means of communication are in the reach of all. In the best books, great men talk to us, give us their most precious thoughts, and pour their souls into ours.
~ *William Ellery Channing 1780-1842, American Unitarian Minister*

God be thanked for books; they are the voices of the distant and the dead, and make us heirs of the spiritual life of past ages.
~ *William Ellery Channing 1780-1842, American Unitarian Minister*

Buy good books, and read them; the best books are the commonest, and the last editions are always the best, if the editors are not blockheads.
~ *Lord Chesterfield 1694-1773, British Statesman*

A good novel tells us the truth about it's hero; but a bad novel tells us the truth about its author.
~ *Gilbert K. Chesterton 1874-1936, British Author*

A book is the only immortality.
~ *Rufus Choate 1799-1859, American Lawyer, Statesman*

I used to walk to school with my nose buried in a book.
~ *Coolio 1963-, American Musician, Rapper, Actor, Singer, Songwriter*

Next to acquiring good friends, the best acquisition is that of good books.
~ *Charles Caleb Colton 1780-1832, British Sportsman Writer*

Many books require no thought from those who read them, and for a very simple reason: they made no such demand upon those who wrote them. Those works, therefore, are the most valuable, that set our thinking faculties in the fullest operation. understand them.
~ *Clarendon*

Books, like friends, should be few and well chosen. Like friends, too, we should return to them again and again for, like true friends, they will never fail us ~ never cease to instruct ~ never cloy.
~ *Charles Caleb Colton 1780-1832, British Sportsman Writer*

The successful Accelerated Reader is able to read larger than normal "blocks" or "bites" of the printed page with each eye stop. He has accepted, without reservation, the philosophy that the most important benefit of reading is the gaining of information, ideas, mental "picture" and entertainment-not the fretting over words. He has come to the realization that words in and of themselves are for the most part insignificant.
~ *Wade E. Cutler*

There is more treasure in books than in all the pirates loot on Treasure Island and best of all, you can enjoy these riches every day of your life.
~ *Walt Disney 1901-1966, American Artist, Film Producer*

Books should to one of these fours ends conduce, for wisdom, piety, delight, or use.
~ *Sir John Denham 1615-1668, British Poet, Dramatist*

A good book is the very essence of a good man. His virtues survive in it, while the foibles and faults of his actual life are forgotten. All the goodly company of the excellent and great sit around my table, or look down on me from yonder shelves, waiting patiently to answer my questions and enrich me with their wisdom. A precious book is a foretaste of immortality.
~ *Theodore L. Cuyler 1822-1909, American Pastor, Author*

The reading of all good books is like a conversation with all the finest men of past centuries.
~ *Rene Descartes 1596-1650, French Philosopher, Scientist*

There are books of which the backs and covers are by far the best parts.
~ *Charles Dickens 1812-1870, British Novelist*

He ate and drank the precious Words, his Spirit grew robust; He knew no more that he was poor, nor that his frame was Dust.
~ *Emily Dickinson 1830-1886, American Poet*

There is no Frigate like a book to take us lands away nor any coursers like a page of prancing Poetry.
~ *Emily Dickinson 1830-1886, American Poet*

I always like to look on the optimistic side of life, but I am realistic enough to know that life is a complex matter.
~ *Walt Disney 1901-1966, American Artist, Film Producer*

Nine-tenths of the existing books are nonsense and the clever books are the refutation of that nonsense.
~ *Benjamin Disraeli 1804-1881, British Statesman, Prime Minister*

Books are fatal: they are the curse of the human race. Nine-tenths of existing books are nonsense, and the clever books are the refutation of that nonsense. The greatest misfortune that ever befell man was the invention of printing.
~ *Benjamin Disraeli 1804-1881, British Statesman, Prime Minister*

A person of mature years and ripe development, who is expecting nothing from literature but the corroboration and renewal of past ideas, may find satisfaction in a lucidity so complete as to occasion no imaginative excitement, but young and ambitious students are not content with it. They seek the excitement because they are capable of the growth that it accompanies.
~ *Charles Horton Cooley 1864-1929, American Sociologist*

Never read any book that is not a year old.
~ *Ralph Waldo Emerson 1803-1882, American Poet, Essayist*

You will, I am sure, agree with me that... if page 534 only finds us in the second chapter, the length of the first one must have been really intolerable.
~ *Sir Arthur Conan Doyle 1859-1930, British Author, "Sherlock Holmes"*

No story is the same to us after a lapse of time; or rather we who read it are no longer the same interpreters.
~ *George Eliot 1819-1880, British Novelist*

Readers are less and less seen as mere non-writers, the subhuman "other" or flawed derivative of the author; the lack of a pen is no longer a shameful mark of secondary status but a positively enabling space, just as within every writer can be seen to lurk, as a repressed but contaminating antithesis, a reader.
~ *Terry Eagleton 1943-, British Critic*

The good of a book lies in its being read. A book is made up of signs that speak of other signs, which in their turn speak of things. Without an eye to read them, a book contains signs that produce no concepts; therefore it is dumb.
~ *Umberto Eco 1929-, Italian Novelist and critic*

We should be as careful of the books we read, as of the company we keep. The dead very often have more power than the living.
~ *Tryon Edwards 1809-1894, American Theologian*

We are too civil to books. For a few golden sentences we will turn over and actually read a volume of four or five hundred pages.
~ *Ralph Waldo Emerson 1803-1882, American Poet, Essayist*

'Tis the good reader that makes the good book; in every book he finds passages which seem to be confidences or sides hidden from all else and unmistakably meant for his ear; the profit of books is according to the sensibility of the reader; the profound thought or passion sleeps as in a mine, until it is discovered by an equal mind and heart.
~ *Ralph Waldo Emerson 1803-1882, American Poet, Essayist*

If we encounter a man of rare intellect, we should ask him what books he reads.
~ *Ralph Waldo Emerson 1803-1882, American Poet, Essayist*

Books are the best of things if well used; if abused, among the worst. They are good for nothing but to inspire. I had better never see a book than be warped by its attraction clean out of my own orbit, and made a satellite instead of a system.
~ *Ralph Waldo Emerson 1803-1882, American Poet, Essayist*

Some books leave us free and some books make us free.
~ *Ralph Waldo Emerson 1803-1882, American Poet, Essayist*

When I get a little money, I buy books; and if any is left I buy food and clothes.
~ *Desiderius Erasmus c.1466-1536, Dutch Humanist*

When you reread a classic, you do not see more in the book than you did before; you see more in you than there was before.
~ *Cliff Fadiman American Writer*

The tools I need for my work are paper, tobacco, food, and a little whiskey.
~ *William Faulkner 1897-1962, American Novelist*

We are as liable to be corrupted by books, as by companions.
~ *Henry Fielding 1707-1754, British Novelist, Dramatist*

Read in order to live.
~ *Gustave Flaubert 1821-1880, French Novelist*

One always tends to overpraise a long book, because one has got through it.
~ *Edward M. Forster 1879-1970, British Novelist, Essayist*

I suggest that the only books that influence us are those for which we are ready, and which have gone a little further down our particular path than we have yet got ourselves.
~ *Edward M. Forster 1879-1970, British Novelist, Essayist*

The only books that influence us are those for which we are ready, and which have gone a little farther down our particular path than we have yet got ourselves.
~ *Edward M. Forster 1879-1970, British Novelist, Essayist*

The books that everybody admires are those that nobody reads.
~ *Anatole France 1844-1924, French Writer*

No tears in the writer, no tears in the reader.
~ *Robert Frost 1875-1963, American Poet*

I don't think any good book is based on factual experience. Bad books are about things the writer already knew before he wrote them.
~ *Carlos Fuentes 1928-, Mexican Novelist, Short-Story Writer*

A book that is shut is but a block.
~ *Thomas Fuller 1608-1661, British Clergyman, Author*

It does not follow because many books are written by persons born in America that there exists an American literature. Books which imitate or represent the thoughts and life of Europe do not constitute an American literature. Before such can exist, an original idea must animate this nation and fresh currents of life must call into life fresh thoughts along the shore.
~ *Margaret Fuller 1810-1850, American Writer, Lecturer*

Books are those faithful mirrors that reflect to our mind the minds of sages and heroes.
~ *Edward Gibbon 1737-1794, British Historian*

My early and invincible love of reading I would not exchange for all the riches of India.
~ *Edward Gibbon 1737-1794, British Historian*

As writers become more numerous, it is natural for readers to become more indolent; whence must necessarily arise a desire of attaining knowledge with the greatest possible ease.
~ *Oliver Goldsmith 1728-1774, Anglo-Irish Author, Poet, Playwright*

I read part of it all the way through.
~ *Samuel Goldwyn 1882-1974, American Film Producer, Founder*

Learning to read has been reduced to a process of mastering a series of narrow, specific, hierarchical skills. Where armed-forces recruits learn the components of a rifle or the intricacies of close order drill "by the numbers," recruits to reading learn its mechanics sound by sound and word by word.
~ *Jacquelyn Gross*

The unread story is not a story; it is little black marks on wood pulp. The reader, reading it, makes it live: a live thing, a story.
~ *Ursula K. Le Guin 1929-, American Author*

In a real sense, people who have read good literature have lived more than people who cannot or will not read. It is not true that we have only one life to live; if we can read, we can live as many more lives and as many kinds of lives as we wish.
~ *S. I. Hayakawa 1902-1992, Canadian Born American Senator*

Thank you for sending me a copy of your book ~ I'll waste no time reading it.
~ *Moses Hadas 1900-1966, American Classicist and Translator*

If I have not read a book before, it is, for all intents and purposes, new to me whether it was printed yesterday or three hundred years ago.
~ *William Hazlitt 1778-1830, British Essayist*

All good books are alike in that they are truer than if they had really happened and after you are finished reading one you will feel that all that happened to you and afterwards it all belongs to you; the good and the bad, the ecstasy, the remorse, and sorrow, the people and the places and how the weather was.
~ *Ernest Hemingway 1898-1961, American Writer*

The good parts of a book may be only something a writer is lucky enough to overhear or it may be the wreck of his whole damn life and one is as good as the other.
~ *Ernest Hemingway 1898-1961, American Writer*

The most foolish kind of a book is a kind of leaky boat on the sea of wisdom; some of the wisdom will get in anyhow.
~ *Oliver Wendell Holmes 1809-1894, American Author, Wit, Poet*

Old books, you know well, are books of the world's youth, and new books are the fruits of its age.
~ *Oliver Wendell Holmes 1809-1894, American Author, Wit, Poet*

The books we read should be chosen with great care, that they may be, as an Egyptian king wrote over his library, "The medicines of the soul."
~ *Paxton Hood*

Be as careful of the books you read, as of the company you keep; for your habits and character will be as much influenced by the former as by the latter.
~ *Paxton Hood*

My books kept me from the ring, the dog-pit, the tavern, and the saloon.
~ *Thomas Hood 1799-1845, British Poet and Humorist*

The mortality of all inanimate things is terrible to me, but that of books most of all.
~ *William Dean Howells 1837-1920, American Novelist, Critic*

This will never be a civilized country until we expend more money for books than we do for chewing gum.
~ *Elbert Hubbard 1859-1915, American Author, Publisher*

I cannot live without books.
~ *Thomas Jefferson 1743-1826, Third President of the USA*

To learn to read is to light a fire; every syllable that is spelled out is a spark.
~ *Victor Hugo 1802-1885, French Poet, Dramatist, Novelist*

It is from books that wise people derive consolation in the troubles of life.
~ *Victor Hugo 1802-1885, French Poet, Dramatist, Novelist*

It is books that teach us to refine our pleasures when young, and to recall them with satisfaction when we are old.
~ *Leigh Hunt 1784-1859, British Poet, Essayist*

A bad book is as much of a labor to write as a good one; it comes as sincerely from the author's soul.
~ *Aldous Huxley 1894-1963, British Author*

Books are the money of Literature, but only the counters of Science.
~ *Thomas H. Huxley 1825-1895, British Biologist, Educator*

The only obligation to which in advance we may hold a novel, without incurring the accusation of being arbitrary, is that it be interesting.
~ *Henry James 1843-1916, American Author*

A man ought to read just as his inclination leads him; for what he reads as a task will do him little good.
~ *Samuel Johnson 1709-1784, British Author*

What is written without effort is in general read without pleasure.
~ *Samuel Johnson 1709-1784, British Author*

You will be the same person in five as you are today except for the people you meet and the books you read.
~ *Charles "Tremendous" Jones American Motivational Speaker, Author*

There was a time when the world acted on books; now books act on the world.
~ *Joseph Joubert 1754-1824, French Moralist*

One man is as good as another until he has written a book.
~ *Benjamin Jowett 1817-1893, British Scholar*

To sit alone in the lamplight with a book spread out before you hold intimate converse with men of unseen generations ~ such is pleasure beyond compare.
~ *Yoshida Kenko*

Except a living man there is nothing more wonderful than a book! a message to us from the dead ~ from human souls we never saw, who lived, perhaps, thousands of miles away. And yet these, in those little sheets of paper, speak to us, arouse us, terrify us, teach us, comfort us, open their hearts to us as brothers.
~ *Charles Kingsley 1819-1875, British Author, Clergyman*

He has left off reading altogether, to the great improvement of his originality.
~ *Charles Lamb 1775-1834, British Essayist, Critic*

We ought to reverence books; to look on them as useful and mighty things. If they are good and true, whether they are about religion, politics, farming, trade, law, or medicine, they are the message of Christ, the maker of all things ~ the teacher of all truth.
~ *Charles Kingsley 1819-1875, British Author, Clergyman*

I can't bear art that you can walk round and admire. A book should be either a bandit or a rebel or a man in the crowd.
~ *D. H. Lawrence 1885-1930, British Author*

I love to lose myself in other men's minds. When I am not walking, I am reading. I cannot sit and think; books think for me.
~ *Charles Lamb 1775-1834, British Essayist, Critic*

One sheds one's sicknesses in books ~ repeats and presents again one's emotions, to be master of them.
~ *D. H. Lawrence 1885-1930, British Author*

The classics are only primitive literature. They belong to the same class as primitive machinery and primitive music and primitive medicine.
~ *Stephen B. Leacock 1869-1944, Canadian Humorist, Economist*

A vacuum of ideas affects people differently than a vacuum of air, otherwise readers of books would be constantly collapsing.
~ *Georg C. Lichtenberg 1742-1799, German Physicist, Satirist*

Do we write books so that they shall merely be read? Don't we also write them for employment in the household? For one that is read from start to finish, thousands are leafed through, other thousands lie motionless, others are jammed against mouseholes, thrown at rats, others are stood on, sat on, drummed on, have gingerbread baked on them or are used to light pipes.
~ *Georg C. Lichtenberg 1742-1799, German Physicist, Satirist*

There are very many people who read simply to prevent themselves from thinking.
~ *Georg C. Lichtenberg 1742-1799, German Physicist, Satirist*

The things I want to know are in books; my best friend is the man who'll get me a book I ain't read.
~ *Abraham Lincoln 1809-1865, Sixteenth President of the USA*

Reading furnishes the mind only with material for knowledge; it is thinking that makes what we read ours.
~ *John Locke 1632-1704, British Philosopher*

From the moment I picked your book up until I laid it down I was convulsed with laughter. Some day I intend reading it.
~ *Groucho Marx 1895-1977, American Comic Actor*

I would sooner read a timetable or a catalog than nothing at all.
~ *W. Somerset Maugham 1874-1965, British Novelist, Playwright*

What is important is not to be able to read rapidly, but to be able to decide what not to read.
~ *James T. Mccay*

Some men have only one book in them, others a library.
~ *Proverb*

A successful book cannot afford to be more than ten percent new.
~ *Marshall Mcluhan 1911-1980, Canadian Communications Theorist*

A house without books is like a room without windows. No man has a right to bring up his children without surrounding them with books, if he has the means to buy them. It is a wrong to his family. Children learn to read by being in the presence of books. The love of knowledge comes with reading and grows upon it. And the love of knowledge, in a young mind, is almost always a warrant against the inferior excitement of passions and vices.
~ *Horace Mann 1796-1859, American Educator*

The chief knowledge that a man gets from reading books is the knowledge that very few of them are worth reading.
~ *H. L. Mencken 1880-1956, American Editor, Author, Critic*

There are two kinds of books. Those that no one reads and those that no one ought to read.
~ *H. L. Mencken 1880-1956, American Editor, Author, Critic*

A person who publishes a book appears willfully in public with his pants down.
~ *Edna St. Vincent Millay 1892-1950, American Poet*

This is not a book. This is libel, slander, defamation of character. This is not a book, in the ordinary sense of the word. No, this is a prolonged insult, a gob of spit in the face of Art, a kick in the pants to God, Man, Destiny, Time, Love, Beauty... what you will. I am going to sing for you, a little off key perhaps, but I will sing.
~ *Henry Miller 1891-1980, American Author*

All my good reading, you might say, was done in the toilet. There are passages in Ulysses which can be read only in the toilet ~ if one wants to extract the full flavor of their content.
~ *Henry Miller 1891-1980, American Author*

A book is a part of life, a manifestation of life, just as much as a tree or a horse or a star. It obeys its own rhythms, its own laws, whether it be a novel, a play, or a diary. The deep, hidden rhythm of life is always there ~ that of the pulse, the heart beat.
~ *Henry Miller 1891-1980, American Author*

Books are not absolutely dead things, but do contain a certain potency of life in them, to be as active as the soul whose progeny they are; they preserve, as in a vial, the purest efficacy and extraction of the living intellect that bred them.
~ *John Milton 1608-1674, British Poet*

Who kills a man kills a reasonable creature, God's image, but thee who destroys a good book, kills reason itself.
~ *John Milton 1608-1674, British Poet*

For books are not absolutely dead things, but do contain a potency of life in them to be as active as that soul was whose progeny they are; nay, they do preserve as in a vial the purest efficacy and extraction of that living intellect that bred them. I know they are as lively, and as vigorously productive, as those fabulous dragon's teeth; and being sown up and down, may chance to spring up armed men.
~ *John Milton 1608-1674, British Poet*

A good book is the precious life-blood of the master spirit, embalmed and treasured up on purpose for a life beyond.
~ *John Milton 1608-1674, British Poet*

Every abridgement of a good book is a fool abridged.
~ *Michel Eyquem De Montaigne 1533-1592, French Philosopher*

The constant habit of perusing devout books is so indispensable, that it has been termed the oil of the lamp of prayer. Too much reading, however, and too little meditation, may produce the effect of a lamp inverted; which is extinguished by the very excess of that ailment, whose property is to feed it.
~ *Hannah More 1745-1833, British Writer, Reformer, Philanthropist*

You will find most books worth reading are worth reading twice.
~ *John Morely*

Early in the morning, at break of day, in all the freshness and dawn of one's strength, to read a book ~ I call that vicious!
~ *Friedrich Nietzsche 1844-1900, German Philosopher*

The books one reads in childhood, and perhaps most of all the bad and good bad books, create in one's mind a sort of false map of the world, a series of fabulous countries into which one can retreat at odd moments throughout the rest of life, and which in some cases can survive a visit to the real countries which they are supposed to represent.
~ *George Orwell 1903-1950, British Author, "Animal Farm"*

This book is not to be tossed lightly aside, but to be hurled with great force.
~ *Dorothy Parker 1893-1967, American Humorous Writer*

I divide all readers into two classes: those who read to remember and those who read to forget.
~ *William Lyon Phelps*

Much reading is an oppression of the mind, and extinguishes the natural candle, which is the reason of so many senseless scholars in the world.
~ *William Penn 1644-1718, British Religious Leader, Founder of Pennsylvania*

What gunpowder did for war the printing press has done for the mind.
~ *Wendell Phillips 1811-1884, American Reformer, Orator*

No man understands a deep book until he has seen and lived at least part of its contents.
~ *Ezra Pound 1885-1972, American Poet, Critic*

Properly, we should read for power. Man reading should be man intensely alive. The book should be a ball of light in one's hand.
~ *Ezra Pound 1885-1972, American Poet, Critic*

There is no robber worse than a bad book.
~ *Italian Proverb Sayings of Italian Origin*

The gains in education are never really lost. Books may be burned and cities sacked, but truth, like the yearning for freedom, lives in the hearts of humble men.
~ *Franklin Delano Roosevelt (1882 - 1945) US president (32nd)*

The reason why so few good books are written is that so few people who can write know anything.
~ *Walter Bagehot (1826 - 1877) English economist, editor, critic*

Miss a meal if you have to, but don't miss a book.
~ *Jim Rohn*

The American mind, unlike the English, is not formed by books, but, as Carl Sandburg once said to me, by newspapers and the Bible.
~ *Van Wyck Brooks (1886 - 1963) US, literary critic, historian*

The book you don't read won't help.
~ *Jim Rohn*

I am a writer of books in retrospect. I talk in order to understand; I teach in order to learn.
~ *Robert Frost (1874 - 1963) US poet*

Don't just read the easy stuff. You may be entertained by it, but you will never grow from it.
~ *Jim Rohn*

The books one has written in the past have two surprises in store: one couldn't write them again, and wouldn't want to.
~ *Jean Rostand 1894-1977, French Biologist, Writer*

In the dark colony of night, when I consider man's magnificent capacity for malice, madness, folly, envy, rage, and destructiveness, and I wonder whether we shall not end up as breakfast for newts and polyps, I seem to hear the muffled cries of all the words in all the books with covers closed.
~ *Leo Rosten 1908-1997, Polish Born American Political Scientist*

A book is a version of the world. If you do not like it, ignore it; or offer your own version in return.
~ *Salman Rushdie 1948-, Indian-born British Author*

You should read books like you take medicine, by advice, and not by advertisement.
~ *John Ruskin 1819-1900, British Critic, Social Theorist*

Be sure that you go to the author to get at his meaning, not to find yours.
~ *John Ruskin 1819-1900, British Critic, Social Theorist*

Books are divided into two classes, the books of the hour and the books of all time.
~ *John Ruskin 1819-1900, British Critic, Social Theorist*

How long most people would look at the best book before they would give the price of a large turbot for it?
~ *John Ruskin 1819-1900, British Critic, Social Theorist*

Without books the development of civilization would have been impossible. They are the engines of change, windows on the world, "Lighthouses" as the poet said "erected in the sea of time." They are companions, teachers, magicians, bankers of the treasures of the mind, Books are humanity in print.
~ *Arthur Schopenhauer 1788-1860, German Philosopher*

To buy books would be a good thing if we also could buy the time to read them.
~ *Arthur Schopenhauer 1788-1860, German Philosopher*

Buying books would be a good thing if one could also buy the time to read them in: but as a rule the purchase of books is mistaken for the appropriation of their contents.
~ *Arthur Schopenhauer 1788-1860, German Philosopher*

Reading is equivalent to thinking with someone else's head instead of with one's own.
~ *Arthur Schopenhauer 1788-1860, German Philosopher*

O, let my books be then the eloquence and dumb presages of my speaking breast.
~ *William Shakespeare 1564-1616, British Poet, Playwright, Actor*

Then I thought of reading ~ the nice and subtle happiness of reading ... this joy not dulled by age, this polite and unpunishable vice, this selfish, serene, lifelong intoxication.
~ *Logan Pearsall Smith 1865-1946, Anglo-American Essayist*

No furniture is so charming as books.
~ *Sydney Smith 1771-1845, British Writer, Clergyman*

Live always in the best company when you read.
~ *Sydney Smith 1771-1845, British Writer, Clergyman*

A multitude of books distracts the mind.
~ *Socrates BC 469-399, Greek Philosopher of Athens*

Reading is to the mind what exercise is to the body. It is wholesome and bracing for the mind to have its faculties kept on the stretch.
~ *Sir Richard Steele 1672-1729, British Dramatist, Essayist, Editor*

A book is like a man ~ clever and dull, brave and cowardly, beautiful and ugly. For every flowering thought there will be a page like a wet and mangy mongrel, and for every looping flight a tap on the wing and a reminder that wax cannot hold the feathers firm too near the sun.
~ *John Steinbeck 1902-1968, American Author*

The age of the book is almost gone.
~ *George Steiner 1929-, French-born American Critic, Novelist*

A novel is a mirror carried along a main road.
~ *Henri B. Stendhal 1783-1842, French Writer*

One may as well be asleep as to read for anything but to improve his mind and morals, and regulate his conduct.
~ *Laurence Sterne 1713-1768, British Author*

Digressions, incontestably, are the sunshine; they are the life, the soul of reading! Take them out of this book, for instance, you might as well take the book along with them; one cold external winter would reign in every page of it; restore them to the writer; he steps forth like a bridegroom, bids All-hail; brings in variety, and forbids the appetite to fail.
~ *Laurence Sterne 1713-1768, British Author*

Books are good enough in their own way, but they are a mighty bloodless substitute for life.
~ *Robert Louis Stevenson 1850-1895, Scottish Essayist, Novelist*
Whoever converses among old books will be hard to please among the new.
~ *Sir William Temple 1628-1699, British Diplomat, Essayist*

If a secret history of books could be written, and the author's private thoughts and meanings noted down alongside of his story, how many insipid volumes would become interesting, and dull tales excite the reader!
~ *William M. Thackeray*

To read well, that is, to read true books in a true spirit, is a noble exercise, and one that will task the reader more than any other exercise which the customs of the day esteem. It requires a training such as the athletes underwent, the steady intention almost of the whole life to this object.
~ *Henry David Thoreau 1817-1862, American Essayist, Poet, Naturalist*

Books must be read as deliberately and reservedly as they were written.
~ *Henry David Thoreau 1817-1862, American Essayist, Poet*

I always begin at the left with the opening word of the sentence and read toward the right and I recommend this method.
~ *James Thurber 1894-1961, American Humorist, Illustrator*

An empty book is like an infant's soul, in which anything may be written. It is capable of all things, but containeth nothing. I have a mind to fill this with profitable wonders.
~ *Thomas Traherne 1636-1674, British Clergyman, Poet, Mystic*

Book love... is your pass to the greatest, the purest, and the most perfect pleasure that God has prepared for His creatures.
~ *Anthony Trollope 1815-1882, British Novelist*

A good book is the best of friends, the same today and for ever.
~ *Martin Tupper1810-1889, British Author, Poet, Inventor*

People are much more willing to lend you books than bookcases.
~ *Mark Twain 1835-1910, American Humorist, Writer*

The man who does not read books has no advantage over the man that can not read them.
~ *Mark Twain 1835-1910, American Humorist, Writer*

A classic is something that everybody wants to have read and nobody wants to read.
~ *Mark Twain 1835-1910, American Humorist, Writer*

All the known world, excepting only savage nations, is governed by books.
~ *Voltaire 1694-1778, French Historian, Writer*

A big leather-bound volume makes an ideal razor strap. A thin book is useful to stick under a table with a broken caster to steady it. A large, flat atlas can be used to cover a window with a broken pane. And a thick, old-fashioned heavy book with a clasp is the finest thing in the world to throw at a noisy cat.
~ *Mark Twain 1835-1910, American Humorist, Writer*

How many a man has dated a new era in his life from the reading of a book! The book exists for us, perchance, that will explain our miracles and reveal new ones. The at present unutterable things we may find somewhere uttered.
~ *Henry David Thoreau 1817-1862, American Essayist, Poet, Naturalist*

In any situation, ask yourself: What strengths do I possess that can contribute towards accomplishing something in this situation? Then follow through.
~ *Source Unknown*

Reading the Scriptures is an uplifting experience.
~ *Source Unknown*

Those who do not read are no better off than those who cannot read.
~ *Source Unknown*

The words of my book nothing, the drift of it everything.
~ *Walt Whitman 1819-1892, American Poet*

I wish I could write a beautiful book to break those hearts that are soon to cease to exist: a book of faith and small neat worlds and of people who live by the philosophies of popular songs.
~ *Source Unknown*

It is far better to be silent than merely to increase the quantity of bad books.
~ *Voltaire 1694-1778, French Historian, Writer*

The books we think we ought to read are poky, dull, and dry; The books that we would like to read we are ashamed to buy; The books that people talk about we never can recall; And the books that people give us, oh, they're the worst of all.
~ *Carolyn Wells 1870-1942, American Author*

Books are lighthouses erected in the great sea of time.
~ *Edwin P. Whipple 1819-1886, American Essayist*

Beware you be not swallowed up in books! An ounce of love is worth a pound of knowledge.
~ *John Wesley 1703-1791, British Preacher, Founder of Methodism*

The books that the world calls immoral are the books that show the world its own shame.
~ *Oscar Wilde 1856-1900, British Author, Wit*

There is no such thing as a moral book or an immoral book. Books are well written or badly written. That is all.
~ *Oscar Wilde 1856-1900, British Author, Wit*

The reason a writer writes a book is to forget a book and the reason a reader reads one is to remember it.
~ *Thomas Wolfe 1931-, American Author, Journalist*

Somewhere, everywhere, now hidden, now apparent in whatever is written down, is the form of a human being. If we seek to know him, are we idly occupied?
~ *Virginia Woolf 1882-1941, British Novelist, Essayist*

Thy books should, like thy friends, not many be, yet such wherein men may thy judgment see.
~ *William Wycherley 1640-1716, British Dramatist*

To read too many books is harmful.
~ *Mao Zedong 1893-1976, Founder of Chinese Communist State*

The road to knowledge begins with the turn of the page.
~ *Author Unknown*

Books give us wisdom in words!
~ *Catherine Pulsifer, from Inspirational Book Reviews*

It is a good thing for an uneducated man to read a book of quotations.
~ *Sir Winston Churchill*

When I am reading a book, whether wise or sill, it seems to me to be alive and talking to me.
~ *Swift*

Everyone who know how to read has it in their power to magnify themselves, multiple the ways in which they exist, to make their life full, significant, and interesting.
~ *Aldous Huxley*

The books that help you the most are those which make you think the most.
~ *Theodore Parker*

Books are the ever-burning lamps of accumulated wisdom.
~ *George William Curtis*

The profit of books is according to the sensibility of the reader. The profoundest thought or passion sleeps as in a mine, until an equal mind and heart finds and publishes it.
~ *Ralph Waldo Emerson*

Books are good enough in their own way, but they are a poor substitute for life.
~ *Robert Louis Stevenson*

Men do not understand books until they have a certain amount of life, or at any rate no man understands a deep book, until he has seen and lived at least part of its contents.
~ *Ezra Pound*

That is a good book which is opened with expectation, and closed with delight and profit.
~ *Amos Bronson Alcott*

He who studies books alone will know how things ought to be, and he who studies men will know how they are.
~ *C. C. Colton*

Books are but waste paper unless we spend in action the wisdom we get from thought.
~ *Edward Bulwer-Lytton*

Books are the quietest and most constant of friends and the most patient of teachers.
~ *Charles W. Eliot*

One can live with the thought of one's own death. It is the thought of the death of the words and books that is terrifying for that is the deeper extinction.
~ *Lance Morrow*

The true University of these days is a Collection of Books.
~ *Thomas Carlyle*

My education was the liberty I had to read indiscriminately and all the time, with my eyes hanging out.
~ *Dylan Thomas*

Outside of a dog, a man's best friend is a book. Inside of a dog, it's too dark to read.
~ *Groucho Marx*

Learning hath gained most by those books by which the printers have lost.
~ *Thomas Fuller*

For books are more than books, they are the life, the very heart and core of ages past, the reason why men worked and died, the essence and quintessence of their lives.
~ *Amy Lowell*

The printing press is either the greatest blessing or the greatest curse of modern times, sometimes one forgets which it is.
~ *Sir James M. Barrie*

A novel is never anything,
but a philosophy put into images.
~ *Albert Camus*

The flood of print has turned reading into a process of gulping rather than savoring.
~ *Warren Chappell*

The great American novel has not only already been written, it has already been rejected.
~ *Frank Dane*

I heard his library burned down and both books were destroyed
~ and one of them hadn't even been colored in yet.
~ *John Dawkins*

Books give not wisdom where none was before. But where some is, there reading makes it more.
~ *John Harington*

The pleasure of reading is doubled when one lives with another who shares the same books. Katherine Mansfield Once we have learned to read, meaning of words can somehow register without consciousness.
~ *Anthony Marcel*

The greatest gift is the passion for reading. It is cheap, it consoles, it distracts, it excites, it gives you knowledge of the world and experience of a wide kind. It is a moral illumination.
~ *Elizabeth Hardwick*

Richard McKenna Deep versed in books and shallow in himself.
~ *John Milton*

Old books that have ceased to be of service should no more be abandoned than should old friends who have ceased to give pleasure.
~ *Sir Peregrine Worsthorne*

Man ceased to be an ape, vanquished the ape, on the day the first book was written.
~ *Yevgeny Zamyatin*

It is easier to buy books than to read them, and easier to read them than to absorb them.
~ *William Osler*

Those moments when you feel you want to read something truly beautiful. The eyes make a tour of the library, and there is nothing. Then you decide to take no matter what, and it is full of beautiful things.
~ *Jules Renard*

When I think of all the books still left for me to read, I am certain of further happiness.
~ *Jules Renard*

There are two motives for reading a book: one, that you enjoy it; the other, that you can boast about it.
~ *Bertrand Russell*

Take the book into your two hands and read your eyes out, you will never find what I find.
~ *Ralph Waldo Emerson in Spiritual Laws Essays, First Series*

Every reader exists to ensure for a certain book a modest immortality. Reading is, in this sense, a ritual of rebirth.
~ *Alberto Manguel in The Library at Night*

Some cleric putting a match to her. Neither of them looks happy about it. Once lit, she'll burn like a book, like a book that was ever finished, like a locked-up library.
~ *Margaret Atwood, Saint Joan of Arc on a Postcard in The Door*

But there is no end to the praise of books, to the value of the library. Who shall estimate their influence on our population where all the millions read and write? It is the joy of nations that man can communicate all his thoughts, discoveries and virtues to records that may last for centuries.
~ *Ralph Waldo Emerson in Address at the Opening of Concord Free Public Library*

The words loved me and I loved them in return.
~ *Sonia Sanchez*

The failure to read good books both enfeebles the vision and strengthens our most fatal tendency ~ the belief that here and now is all there is.
~ *Allan Bloom*

From your parents you learn love and laughter and how to put one foot before the other. But when books are opened you discover that you have wings.
~ *Helen Hayes*

In the right hands, literature is not resorted to as a consolation, and by the broken and decayed, but as a decalogue.
~ *Ralph Waldo Emerson*

If the sentences knew how I read them…
~ *Geoffrey O'Brien*

True literature can exist only where it is created, not by diligent and trustworthy officials, but by madmen, hermits, heretics, dreamers, rebels, and skeptics.
~ *Yevgeny Zamyatin*

In the highest civilization the book is still the highest delight. He who has once known its satisfactions is provided with a resource against calamity.
~ *Ralph Waldo Emerson*

Reading is important ~ read between the lines. Don't swallow everything.
~ *Gwendolyn Brooks*

'T is the good reader that makes the good book.
~ *Ralph Waldo Emerson*

No book so bad but some part may be of use.
~ *Pliny*

I think we ought to read only the kind of books that wound and stab us.
~ *Franz Kafka*

My home is where my books are.
~ *Ellen Thompson*

Anyone who has a book collection and a garden wants for nothing.
~ *Marcus Tullius Cicero*

We continue to believe that books embody the ideas that turn us from isolated souls into a powerful community.
~ *Mission Statement of Harry W Schwartz Bookshops*

And indeed, what is better than to sit by one's fireside in the evening with a book, while the wind beats against the window and the lamp is burning?
~ *Gustave Falubert in Madame Bovary*

But he who truly loves books loves all books alike, and not only this, but it grieves him that all other men do not share with him this noble passion. Verily, this is the most unselfish of loves!
~ *Eugene Field in Love Affairs of a Bibliomaniac*

The world is a library of strange and wonderful books, and sometimes we just need to go prowling through the stacks.
~ *Michael Dirda*

Woke up this morning witha terrific urge to lie in bed all day and read.
~ *Raymond Carver*

Income tax returns are the most imaginative fiction being written today.
~ *Herman Wouk*

A collector recently bought at public auction, in London, for one hundred and fifty-seven guineas, an autograph of Shakespeare; but for nothing a school-boy can read Hamlet and can detect secrets of highest concernment yet unpublished therein.
~ *Ralph Waldo Emerson in Experience*

Of course, literature is the only spiritual and humane career. Even painting tends to dumness, and music turns people erotic, whereas the more you write the nicer you become.
~ *Virginia Woolf*

Life is our dictionary.
~ *Ralph Waldo Emerson, The American Scholar*

There is then creative reading as well as creative writing. When the mind is braced by labor and invention, the page of whatever book we read becomes luminous with manifold allusion. Every sentence is doubly significant, and the sense of our author is as broad as the world.
~ *Ralph Waldo Emerson, in The American Scholar*

Literature is my Utopia. Here I am not disenfranchised. No barrier of the senses shuts me out from the sweet, gracious discourse of my book friends. They talk to me without embarrassment or awkwardness.
~ *Helen Keller*

Magazines all too frequently lead to books, and should be regarded by the prudent as the heavy petting of literature.
~ *Fran Lebowitz*

Words! Mere words! How terrible they were! How clear, and vivid and cruel! One could not escape from them. And yet what a subtle magic there was in them! They seemed to be able to give a plastic form to formless things, and to have a music of their own as sweet as that of the viol or lute. Mere words! Was there anything so real as words?
~ *Oscar Wilde in The Picture of Dorian Gray*

A great novel is a kind of conversion experience. We come away from it changed.
~ *Katherine Patterson*

I only read what I am hungry for at the moment when I have an appetite for it, and then I do not read, I eat.
~ *Simone Weil*

The book must of necessity be put into a bookcase. And the bookcase must be housed. And the house must be kept. And the library must be dusted, must be arranged, must be catalogued. What a vista of toil, yet not unhappy toil!
~ *William Gladstone*

I always begin at the left with the opening word of the sentence and read towards the right and I recommend this method.
~ *James Thurber*

What enriches language is its being handled and exploited by beautiful minds ~ not so much by making innovations as by expanding it through more vigorous and varied applications, by extending it and deploying it. It is not words that they contribute: what they do is enrich their words, deepen their meanings and tie down their usage; they teach it unaccustomed rhythms, prudently though and with ingenuity.
~ *Michel de Montaigne, On Some Lines of Virgil*

Comerado, this is no book, Who touches this, touches a man,(Is it night? Are we here alone?)It is I you hold, and who holds you, I spring from the pages into your arms ~ decease calls me forth.
~ *Walt Whitman, Leaves of Grass*

Books must be read as deliberately and as reservedly as they were written.
~ *Henry David Thoreau*

Second-hand books are wild books, homeless books; they have come together in vast flocks of variegated feather, and have a charm which the domesticated volumes of the library lack. Besides, in this random miscellaneous company we may rub against some complete stranger who will, with luck, turn into the best friend we have in the world.
~ *Virginia Woolf*

In some respects the better a book is, the less it demands from the binding.
~ *Charles Lamb*

We agreed that people are now afraid of the English language. He [T.S. Eliot] said it came of being bookish, but not reading books enough. One should read all styles thoroughly.
~ *Virginia Woolf from The Diary of Virginia Woolf*

There are those who, while reading a book, recall, compare, conjure up emotions from other, previous readings. This is one of the most delicate forms of adultery.
~ *Ezequiel Martínez Estrada*

Tough choices face the biblioholic at every step of the way ~ like choosing between reading and eating, between buying new clothes and buying books, between a reasonable lifestyle and one of penurious but masochistic happiness lived out in the wallow of excess.
~ *Tom Raabe, Biblioholism: The Literary Addiction*

I seldom read on beaches or in gardens. You can't read by two lights at once, the light of day and the light of the book. You should read by electric light, the room in shadow, and only the page lit up.
~ *Marguerite Duras*

Our true birthplace is that in which we cast for the first time an intelligent eye on ourselves. My first homelands were my books.
~ *Marguerite Yourcenar*

It is not true that we have only one life to live; if we can read, we can live as many more lives and as many kinds of lives as we wish.
~ *S.I. Hiyakawa*

Poets are never allowed to be mediocre by the gods, by men or by publishers.
~ *Horace as quoted by Montaigne*

Books are carriers of civilization. Without books, history is silent, literature dumb, science crippled, thought and speculations at a standstill.
~ *Barbara W. Tuchman*

All my life I have been trying to learn to read, to see and hear, and to write.
~ *Carl Sandburg*

The dear good people don't know how long it takes to learn to read. I've been at it eighty years, and can't say yet that I've reached the goal.
~ *Johann Wolfgang von Goethe*

A home without books is a body without soul.
~ *Marcus Tullius Cicero*

[To] turn poet, they say, is an infectious and incurable distemper.
~ *Cervantes, Don Quixote, I, 6*

The smallest bookstore still contains more ideas of worth than have been presented in the entire history of television.
~ *Andrew Ross*

A book reads the better which is our own, and has been so long known to us, that we know the topography of its blots, and dog's ears, and can trace the dirt in it to having read it at tea with buttered muffins.
~ *Charles Lamb*

Time comes into it. Say it. Say it. The universe is made of stories, not of atoms.
~ *Muriel Rukeyser, The Speed of Darkness*

Books open your mind, broaden your mind, and strengthen you as nothing else can.
~ *William Feather*

You know you've read a good book when you turn the last page and feel a little as if you have lost a friend.
~ *Paul Sweeney*

Do not consider it proof just because it is written in books, for a liar who will deceive with his tongue will not hesitate to do the same with his pen.
~ *Maimonides*

Books support us in our solitude and keep us from being a burden to ourselves.
~ *Jeremy Collier*

If in other lands the press and books and literature of all kinds are censored, we must redouble our efforts here to keep them free.
~ *Franklin D. Roosevelt*

We will open the book. Its pages are blank. We are going to put words on them ourselves. The book is called Opportunity and its first chapter is New Year's Day.
~ *Edith Lovejoy Pierce*

When I get a little money I buy books; and if any is left I buy food and clothes.
~ *Desiderius Erasmus*

A house without books is like a room without windows. No man has a right to bring up his children without surrounding them with books, if he has the means to buy them.
~ *Horace Mann*

Reading history is good for all of us, he says, not surprisingly, perhaps, but his rationale is a fresh, somewhat bracing thought: If you know history, you know that there is no such thing as a self-made man or self-made woman. We are shaped by people...
~ *David C. McCullough*

When you reread a classic, you do not see more in the book than you did before; you see more in you than there was before.
~ *Cliff Fadiman*

My personal hobbies are reading, listening to music, and silence.
~ *Bernie Hubley*

Books are humanity in print.
~ *Barbara W. Tuchman*

Books are the carriers of civilization. Without books, history is silent, literature dumb, science crippled, thought and speculation at a standstill.
~ *Barbara W. Tuchman*

We shouldn't teach great books; we should teach a love of reading.
~ *B. F. Skinner*

Don`t join the book burners. Don`t think you`re going to conceal faults by concealing evidence that they ever existed. Don`t be afraid to go in your library and read every book...
~ *Andy Gates*

A good book is the precious life-blood of a master spirit, embalmed and treasured up on purpose to a life beyond life.
~ *John Milton, Areopagitica*

Books are not absolutely dead things, but do contain a potency of life in them to be as active as that soul was whose progeny they are; nay they do preserve as in a vial the purest efficacy and extraction of that living intellect that bred them.
~ *John Milton, Areopagitica*

A man who keeps a diary pays,
Due toll to many tedious days;
But life becomes eventful—then,
His busy hand forgets the pen.
Most books, indeed, are records less
Of fullness than of emptiness.
~ *William Allingham, A Diary*

Books are not seldom talismans and spells.
~ *William Cowper, The Task*

What traitors books can be! You think they're backing you up, and they turn on you. Others can use them, too, and there you are, lost in the middle of the moor, in a great welter of nouns and verbs and adjectives.
~ *Ray Bradbury, Fahrenheit 451*

Prolonged, indiscriminate reviewing of books is a quite exceptionally thankless, irritating and exhausting job. It not only involves praising trash but constantly inventing reactions towards books about which one has no spontaneous feeling whatever.
~ *George Orwell, Confessions of a Book Reviewer*

'Tis the good reader that makes the good book.
~ *Ralph Waldo Emerson, Society and Solitude*

Books are my friends, my companions. They make me laugh and cry and find meaning in life.
~ *Christopher Laolini, Eragon*

What I look for most in the books I read is a sense of consciousness. It's so I know that I've lived. At the end, I can say, Yes, I have been here~ I was here, and I was paying attention.
~ *Lili Taylor, O Magazine, Aug. 2006*

I'm much more willing to buy a novel electronically by someone I don't know. Because if halfway through I think, I don't really like this, I can just stop. I can't throw books out, even if I think they're crummy. I feel like I've got to give it to the library. I've got to loan it to somebody, or I keep it on my shelf. It's like a plant.
~ *Susan Orlean, Newsweek, Jul. 13, 2009*

A good book is the purest essence of a human soul.
~ *Thomas Carlyle, speech in support of the London Library, 1840*

Books were the sustenance of God. And His munitions.
~ *Regis Debray, God: An Itinerary*

After all, one of the reasons there are lots of books in bookstores is that you don't have to buy the books you don't want.
~ *Salman Rushdie, January Magazine interview, 2002*

Anyhow, kids are very tough. What they find for themselves they should be able to read for themselves.
~ *Ursula K. LeGuin, Horn Book letter, 1973*

Are there not moments,' he asked William, 'when you would also do shameful things to get your hands on a book you have been seeking for years?
~ *Umberto Eco, The Name of the Rose. HBJ, 1983*

Be careful of reading health books. You may die of a misprint.
~ *Mark Twain*

Depending on whichever book you read
Sometimes it takes a lifetime to get what you need
~ *Aimee Mann, Mr. Harris*

Don't Judge a Book by Its Video Case.
~ *Julie Larson, The Dinette Set comic strip, 2002*

A book worth reading is worth buying.
~ *John Ruskin 1819-1900, British Critic, Social Theorist*

Don't you know that those old musty books, as you call them, are the only things worth anything in all this library? All the rest is trash.
~ *Saxe Holm, Mrs. Millington and Her Librarian.*
*A Love Story (Harper's New Monthly Magazine, June 1881, p. 109)*

He liked books if they were books of information and had pictures of grain elevators or of fat foreign children doing exercises in model schools.
~ *C.S. Lewis The Voyage of the Dawn Treader*

I believe that today more than ever a book should be sought after even if it has only one great page in it: we must search for fragments, splinters, toenails, anything that has ore in it, anything that is capable of resuscitating the body and soul.
~ *Henry Miller*

I didn't lie! I was writing fiction with my mouth!
~ *The Simpsons, Diatribe of a Mad Housewife episode, 2004.*

It doesn't cost any more to print something true than it does to print crap.
~ *Melvin Burgess (Losing It. Andersen Press, 2003, p. 254 ~ as quoted in review by Anne Fine)*

I should have listened to the almanac.
It said that I should stay in bed.
~ *Off Broadway (Full Moon Turn My Head Around)*

Is this where they keep the philostophers now, with the rugs and the dust, where the books go to die?
~ *Frank Zappa, The Adventures of Greggery Peccary*

If this book be false in its facts, disprove them; if false in its reasoning, refute it. But, for God's sake, let us freely hear both sides, if we choose.
~ *Thomas Jefferson, 1814*

I would be most content if my children grew up to be the kind of people who think decorating consists mostly of building enough bookshelves.
~ *Anna Quindlen, Enough Bookshelves, New York Times, 7 August 1991*

Let books be your dining table,
And you shall be full of delights
Let them be your mattress
And you shall sleep restful nights
~ *St. Ephrem the Syrian (303-373) Quoted in Bar Hebraues' Ethicon*

It is this author's devout hope that in time he may be able to produce acceptable books about cute furry animals and ~ for the older reader ~ stories about high schools in California with really good athletic programs and uniformly attractive students. In the meantime, while the sort of adumbrated and sinister production which follows these remarks continues to issue forth (to my considerable enrichment ~ and the publisher's), the least I can do is to entreat teachers and librarians of the better sort to keep the book out of the hands of the young.
~ *Daniel M. Pinkwater, Young Adults. Tor, 1985*

It's a good thing when children enjoy books, isn't it?
~ *Judy Blume (New York Times article, 22 October 1999)*

It's called freedom of choice, and it's one of the principles this country was founded upon. Look it up in the library, Reverend, if you have any of them left when you've finished burning all the books.
~ *George Carlin*

'One can never have enough socks, said Dumbledore. 'Another Christmas has come and gone and I didn't get a single pair. People will insist on giving me books.'
~ *J.K. Rowling (Harry Potter and the Sorcerer's Stone)*

Other shelves were full of books. They were the only things in the room that looked as though they had never been touched.
~ *J.K. Rowling (Harry Potter and the Sorcerer's Stone. Scholastic, 1997, pp. 37-38)*

So this is a bookstore ... smells boring.
~ *King of the Hill episode. (Line spoken by the character of Dale)*

Somehow reading a book never feels like sitting still.
~ *Jef Mallett (Frazz comic strip, 16 January 2004. Line spoken by the title character.)*

The greatest threat to the book is not the computer. It is the censor.
~ *Anna Quindlen (PLA keynote address, 25 February 2004)*

Volumes have secrets. Take them on holiday.
Book them a room, save them a moment.
~ *The Church (Volumes ~ Submitted by Marylaine Block)*

There is a magic in some books
That sucks a man into connections
With the spirits hard to touch
That join him to his kind.
~ *Roger Waters*

There you sit, sitting spare like a book on a shelf, rusting.
~ *Led Zeppelin (Misty Mountain Hop)*

They say that reading is dead, but it isn't. It's just ... uh ... pathologically crippled.
~ *Jon Stewart (The Daily Show, 14 July 2004)*

Until one has some kind of professional relationship with books, one does not discover how bad the majority of them are.
~ *George Orwell (Submitted by M.J.B. of Brazil)*

We've taken care of everything.
The words you read, the songs you sing.
The pictures that give pleasure to your eye.
~ *Rush (2112)*

You're a torn-out page from a bestselling book.
~ *Jeff Beck (Peaches and Cream)*

With my eyes closed, I would touch a familiar book and draw its fragrance deep inside me. This was enough to make me happy.
~ *Haruki Murakami (Norwegian Wood. Vintage, 2000, p. 30)*

Yeah, they caught him in the library reading a book. Freak.
~ *Grounded for Life episode, 24 January 2001, line spoken by*

You are the dumbest, maddest man I've met. That's what I get for putting you on to books.
~ *Luciano Vincenzoni and Sergio Donati (Orca, 1977. Line spoken by Charlotte Rampling as Rachel Bedford)*

You knew I'd wanna read it. ... You're a book tease.
*(Gilmore Girls episode, line spoken by Milo Ventimiglio as Jess)*

You teach a child to read, and he or her will be able to pass a literacy test.
~ *George W. Bush (Speaking at Townsend Elementary School, near Knoxville TN, 21 February 2001)*

A book is the only place in which you can examine a fragile thought without breaking it, or explore an explosive idea without fear it will go off in your face. It is one of the few havens remaining where a man's mind can get both provocation and privacy.
~ *Edward P. Morgan*

Many people, other than the authors, contribute to the making of a book, from the first person who had the bright idea of alphabetic writing through the inventor of movable type to the lumberjacks who felled the trees that were pulped for its printing. It is not customary to acknowledge the trees themselves, though their commitment is total.
~ *Forsyth and Rada*

The greatest gift is a passion for reading. It is cheap, it consoles, it distracts, it excites, it gives you the knowledge of the world and experience of a wide kind. It is a moral illumination.
~ *Elizabeth Hardwick*

A book lying idle on a shelf is wasted ammunition. Like money, books must be kept in constant circulation. Lend and borrow to the maximum ~ of both books and money! But especially books, for books represent infinitely more than money. A book is not only a friend, it makes friends for you. When you have possessed a book with mind and spirit, you are enriched. But when you pass it on you are enriched threefold.
~ *Henry Miller*

We have preserved the Book, and the Book has preserved us.
~ *David Ben-Gurion*

All humanity is passion: without passion, religion, history, novels, art would be ineffectual.
~ *Honoré de Balzac*

It's a feature of our age that if you write a work of fiction, everyone assumes that the people and events in it are disguised biography — but if you write your biography, it's equally assumed you're lying your head off.
~ *Margaret Atwood, On Writing Poetry Wales, June 1995*

But the feeling I have, you know, is that I'll never come close to reading all, or even a thousandth- a billionth- of the books I'd probably love if I ever got to them.
~ *Dave Barry*, Shwartz, *Ronald B. For the Love of Books: Grosset/Putnam. New York: 1999.*

I grew up in a small town with a very small library. But the books in the library opened a large place in my heart. It is the place where stories live. And those stories have been informing my days, comforting my nights, and extending possibilities ever since. If that library had not been there, if the books ~ such as they were ~ had not been free, my world would be poor, even today.

*~ Marion Dane Bauer, American Library Association. Books Change Lives: Quotes to Treasure. Booklist Publications: 1994.*

## Two Lives Are Yours

Books I think
Are extra nice.
Through books you live
Not once but twice.
You are yourself
And you are things
With fur or fins
Or shells or wings,
As big as giants,
Small as gnats,
As far as stars
As close as cats.

You live today
And long ago.
The future, too,
Is yours to know.

You're multiplied,
Expanded, freed.
You're you and also
What you read.
~ *Richard Armour 1973.*

Someone said, the dead writers are remote from us because we know so much more than they did. Precisely, and they are that which we know.
~ *T.S. Eliot*

The computer can help us find what we know is there. But the book remains our symbol and our resource for the unimagined question and the unwelcome answer.
~ *Daniel J. Boorstin, Cole, John Y. In Memoriam: Daniel J. Boorstin.*

All the glory of the world would be buried in oblivion, unless God had provided mortals with the remedy of books.
~ *Richard de Bury, The Love of Books: The Philobiblon. 1345. Translated by E. C. Thomas. De La More Press, London: 1903.*

The truth is that every book we read, like every person we meet, has the capacity to change our lives. And though we can be sure our children will meet people, we must, must create, these days, their chance to meet books.
~ *Susan Cooper, Books Change Lives: Quotes to Treasure 1994.*

Reading maketh a full man.
~ *Sir Francis Bacon, Of Studies 1597*

Let my temptation be a book.
~ *Eugene Field, The Love Affairs of a Bibliomaniac. IndyPublish.com: 2002.*

The book must be an ice-axe to break the seas frozen inside our soul.
~ *Franz Kafka*

Reading is to the mind what exercise is to the body. It is wholesome and bracing for the mind to have its faculties kept of the stretch.
~ *Augustus Hare*

The printed page illuminates the mind of a man and defies, as afar as anything sublimary can, the corrosive hand of time.
~ *Denys Hay, Bettman, Otto L. The Delights of Reading: Quotes, Notes, & Anecdotes. David R. Godine, Publisher, Inc. Boston: 1987.*

The love of learning, the sequestered nooks,
And all the sweet serenity of books.
~ *Henry Wadsworth Longfellow, Morituri salutamus 1875*

Ten guards and the warden couldn't have torn me out of those books. Months passed without even thinking about being imprisoned....I had never been so truly free in my life.
~ *Malcolm X (Malcolm Little), Civil Rights Activist, 1925-1965*

I must say that I find television very educational. The minute somebody turns it on, I go to the library and read a book.
~ *Groucho Marx, American comedian. 1890-1977*

Once upon a time in the dead of winter in the Dakota Territory, Theodore Roosevelt took off in a makeshift boat down the Little Missouri River in pursuit of a couple of thieves who had stolen his prized rowboat. After several days on the river, he caught up and got the draw on them with his trusty Winchester, at which point they surrendered. Then Roosevelt set off in a borrowed wagon to haul the thieves cross-country to justice. They headed across the snow-covered wastes of the Badlands to the railhead at Dickinson, and Roosevelt walked the whole way, the entire 40 miles. It was an astonishing feat, what might be called a defining moment in Roosevelt's eventful life. But what makes it especially

memorable is that during that time, he managed to read all of Anna Karenina. I often think if that when I hear people say they haven't time to read.
~ *David McCullough "No Time to Read"*

The first word Edmund Gosse said was not mama or dada but book.
~ *Tom Raabe, Bilioholism. Fulcrum Publishing. Golden, Colorado: 2001.*

The study period in school. A teacher told me that she whipped a boy for hollerin' in time o' books.
~ *Vance Randolph and George Wilson Randolph, Down in the Holler.*

You know you've read a good book when you turn the last page and feel a little as if you have lost a friend.
~ *Paul Sweeney*

Books are the carriers of civilization. Without books, history is silent, literature dumb, science crippled, thought and speculation at a standstill.
~ *Barbara W. Tuchman*

I conceive that a knowledge of books is the basis on which all other knowledge rests.
~ *George Washington, First American president. 1732-1799*

## I am the book

I'll be your friend,
stay by your side,
contradict you,
make you laugh or teary-eyed,
On a sun-summer morning.

I'll spark you,
help you sleep,
bring dreams
you'll forever keep
On a dappled-autumn afternoon.

I'll warm you,
keep you kindled,
dazzle you,
till storms have dwindled
On a snow-flaked winter evening.

I'll plant you,
a spring-seeding
with bursting life
while you are reading.

I am the book
you are needing.
~ *Tom Robert Shields*

The man who does not read books has not advantage over the man who can't read them.
~ *Mark Twain, American humorist and writer 1835-1910.*

Poetry and Hums aren't things which you get, they're things which get you.
~ *Winnie the Pooh*

If a man can write a better book, preach a better sermon, or make a better mousetrap, than his neighbor, though he build his house in the woods, the world will make a beaten path to his door.
~ *Ralph Waldo Emerson*

Some books are undeservedly forgotten, none are undeservedly remembered.
~ *W.H. Auden*

A room without a book is like a body without a soul.
~ *Marcus Tullius Cicero*

I suggest that the only books that influence us are those for which we are ready, and which have gone a little further down our particular path than we have gone ourselves.
~ *E. M. Forster*

The books that the world calls immoral are the books that show the world own shame.
~ *Oscar Wilde*

Life-transforming ideas have always come to me through books.
~ *Bell Hooks*

There is more treasure in books than in all the pirate's loot on Treasure Island ... and best of all, you can enjoy these riches every day of your life.
~ *Walt Disney*

A house without books is like a room without windows.
~ *Horace Mann*

Books, the children of the brain.
~ *Jonathan Swift*

Motherhood is like Albania ~ you can't trust the descriptions in the books, you have to go there.
~ *Marni Jackson*

When I am dead, I hope it is said, 'His sins were scarlet, but his books were read'.
~ *Hillaire Belloc*

I have fallen in love a thousand times in my lifetime. All which have been with books.
~ *Unknown*

The things I want to know are in books; my best friend is the man who'll get me a book I ain't read.
~ *Abraham Lincoln (1809-1865)*

Choose your friends like your books, few but choice.
~ *American Proverb*

It is far better to be silent than merely to increase the quantity of bad books.
~ *Voltaire [Francois-Marie Arouet]*

It had been startling and disappointing to me to find out that story books had been written by people, that books were not natural wonders, coming of themselves like grass.
~ *Eudora Welty, US author 1909-*

These are not books, lumps of lifeless paper, but minds alive on the shelves.
~ *Gilbert Highet*

The covers of this book are too far apart.
~ *Ambrose Bierce*

It is a good thing for an uneducated man to read books of quotations.
~ *Sir Winston Churchill*

Good friends, good books and a sleepy conscience: this it the ideal life.
~ *Mark Twain*

Imagine a survivor of a failed civilization with only a tattered book on aromatherapy for guidance in arresting a cholera epidemic. Yet, such a book would more likely be found amid the debris than a comprehensible medical text.
~ *James Lovelock*

Nobody ever committed suicide while reading a good book, but many have while trying to write one.
~ *Robert Byrne*

Room without books is like a body without a soul.
~ *Marcus Tullius Cicero*

A book of quotations … can never be complete.
~ *Robert M. Hamilton*

Today's public figures can no longer write their own speeches or books, and there is some evidence that they can't read them either.
~ *Gore Vidal*

A book must be an ice-axe to break the seas frozen inside our soul.
~ *Franz Kafka (1883-1924) Czech writer*

All a writer has to do to get a woman is to say he's a writer. It's an aphrodisiac.
~ *Saul Bellow*

The writings of the wise are the only riches that our posterity cannot squander.
~ *Walter Savage Landor*

Camerado, this is no book. Who touches this, touches a man.
~ *Walter Whitman*

Byron says that a small drop of ink may make millions think. Many a time a book has decided the character of a man's life. A book makes friends for you; for there springs up from its reading an acquaintanceship not only between you and the author, but between you and another man who reads the same book. Samuel Johnson, hearing that a man had read Burton's Anatomy of Melancholy, exclaimed, If I knew that man I could hug him. It is said that Cæsar, when shipwrecked and in danger of drowning, did not try to save his gold, but took his Commentaries between his teeth and swam to shore.
~ *John Wilson, from a paper read before the Club of Odd Volumes, in Boston.*

Who kills a man kills a reasonable creature, God's image; but he who destroys a good book kills reason itself, kills the image of God, as it were, in the eye.

*~ John Milton John Milton Information at Luminarium.org*

You do not publish your own verses, Laelius; you criticize mine. Pray cease to criticize mine, or else publish your own.

*~ Martial, Roman author*

Books are not made like children but like pyramids ... and they are just as useless! and they stay in the desert! ... Jackals piss at their foot and the bourgeois climb up on them.

*~ Gustave Flaubert*

All books are divisible into two classes: the books of the hour, and the books of all time.

*~ John Ruskin*

A book that furnishes no quotations is, me judice, no book ~ it is a plaything.

*~ Thomas Love Peacock*

Books are good enough in their own way, but they are a poor substitute for life.

*~ Robert Louis Stevenson*

Everything in the world exists in order to end up as a book.

*~ Stephan Mallarme*

Seek ye out of the book of the Lord, and read.

*~ Isaiah 34:16*

The sensation felt when touching paper differs from the coldness of metal or the perfection of plastic as it radiates a core warmth that we expect to come from a living object. Each fiber greets our hands in a comfortable, familiar tradition that we were introduced to as children, and constantly thereafter in school and at work. Most of the paper we use is bleached perfectly white with just enough texture to reliably meet the rubber rollers of a copy machine. Yet once in a while we are fortunate enough to encounter the kind of graphic design that not only visually stimulates, but that we can also taste with.
~ *John Maeda The Reactive Square*

A book is a human-powered film projector (complete with feature film) that advances at a speed fully customized to the viewer's mood or fancy. This rare harmony between object and user arises from the minimal skills required to manipulate a bound sequence of pages. Each piece of paper embodies a corresponding instant of time which remains frozen until liberated by the act of turning a page.
~ *The John Maeda, Reactive Square*

We read about 1,000 times more than we write.
~ *Rich Gold, Xerox PARC*

We think of an eBook as an intelligent pet.
~ *Talan Memmot, BeeHive Hypertext*

Reading surrounds us, labels us, defines us.
~ *Rich Gold, Xerox PARC*

The world is a book, and those who do not travel, read only a page.
~ *St. Augustine*

The age of the book is about gone.
~ *George Steiner*

It took people 10 years to figure out that while stuck in a morning commute, they could be listening to a book.
~ *Paul Hilts, Publishers Weekly*

The illiterate of the 21st century will not be those who cannot read and write, but those who cannot learn, unlearn, and relearn.
~ *Alvin Toffler*

Change can be scary. When papyrus replaced clay tablets, and the Gutenberg press calligraphy, did a bit of panic set in? Are we in the midst of a revolution of similar proportion? Very probably.
~ *Susan McLester*

A popular admonition goes Don't judge a book by its cover. Yet we do it all the time. We ascribe qualities of character to people based on their physical characteristics. And our language takes shape to reflect that attitude.
~ *Anu Garg*

We should not see print and electronic literature as in competition, but rather in conversation. The more voices that join in, the richer the dialogue is likely to be.
~ *N. Katherine Hayles*

Of making many books there is no end, and much study is a weariness of the flesh.
~ *Ecclesiastes 12:12*

The printed page transcends space and time. The printed page, the infinity of the book, must be transcended.
~ *El Lissitzky, The Electro-Library*

Read o'er the volume of young Paris' face,
And find delight writ there with beauty's pen.
Examine every married lineament,
And see how one another lends content,
And what obscured in this fair volume lies
Find written in the margin of his eyes.
This precious book of love, this unbound lover,
To beautify him, only lacks a cover.
The fish lives in the sea, and 'tis much pride
For fair without the fair within to hide.
That book in many's eyes doth share the glory
That in golden clasps locks in the story.
So shall you share all that he doth possess,
By having him making yourself no less.
Lady Capulet talking to Juliet,
compares the young lover's face
to a most captivating book and
invites her to read in it with delight.
~ *William Shakespeare, Romeo and Juliet*

Books are the carriers of civilization... They are companions, teachers, magicians, bankers of the treasures of the mind. Books are humanity in print.
~ *Barbara W. Tuchman*

When you realize the difference between the container and the content, you will have knowledge.
~ *Idries Shah, The Book of the Book*

The body of Benjamin Franklin
Printer,
Like the covering
Of an old book
Its contents torn out
And stript of its lettering
And gilding
Lies here, food for worms;
But the work
Shall not be lost,
It will (as he believed)
Appear once more,
In a new
And more beautiful edition,
Corrected and amended
By the author.
~ *Epitaph for Benjamin Franklin*

Books may well be the only true magic.
~ *Alice Hoffman*

I grew up kissing books and bread.
~ *Salman Rushdie, Imaginary Homelands*

It is with the reading of books the same as with looking at pictures; one must, without doubt, without hesitations, with assurance, admire what is beautiful.
~ *Vincent van Gogh*

Real education consists in drawing the best out of yourself. What better book can there be than the book of humanity?
~ *Mohandas K. Gandhi*

I cannot live without books. In a letter to John Adams.
- *Thomas Jefferson*

What is the use of a book, thought Alice, without pictures or conversations?
~ *Alice's Adventures in Wonderland*

For books are more than books. They are the life, the very heart and core of ages past, the reason why men lived and worked and died, the essence and quintessence of their lives.
~ *Amy Lowell*

If there's a book you really want to read but it hasn't been written yet, then you must write it.
~ *Toni Morrison*

Keep reading books, but remember that a book's only a book, and you should learn to think for yourself.
~ *Maxim Gorky*

I find television very educational. Every time someone turns it on, I go in the other room and read a book.
~ *Groucho Marx*

There is no reason why the same man should like the same books at eighteen and at forty-eight.
~ *Ezra Pound, ABC of Reading*

Only in books has mankind known perfect truth, love and beauty.
~ *George Bernard Shaw*

What in the world would we do without our libraries?
~ *Katharine Hepburn*

I've been drunk for about a week now, and I thought it might sober me up to sit in a library.
~ *F. Scott Fitzgerald, The Great Gatsby*

Wherever they burn books they will also, in the end, burn human beings.
~ *Almansor - Heinrich Heine*

Classic—a book people praise and don't read.
~ *Mark Twain, Following the Equator*

God forbid that any book should be banned. The practice is as indefensible as infanticide.
~ *Rebecca West, The Strange Necessity*

Books cannot be killed by fire. People die, but books never die. No man and no force can take from the world the books that embody man's eternal fight against tyranny. In this war, we know, books are weapons.
~ *Franklin Delano Roosevelt, Message to the American Booksellers Association*

Even bad books are books, and therefore sacred.
~ *Gunther Grass, The Tin Drum*

The portability of the book, like that of the easel painting, added much to the new cult of individualism.
~ *Marshall McLuhan, The Gutenburg Galaxy*

Still, the E-book is not a passing thing, but here to stay as it becomes cheaper and improved. Nonetheless, it is really no more than a screen upon which to read, and it is clear that when enough people start reading them, electronic books will do for the ophthalmologists what taffy and caramels did for dentists.
~ *Martin Arnold, In The New York Times*

Every book is a failure.
~ *George Orwell*

Every man must die sooner or later, but good books must be preserved.
~ Don Vincente

You can never be too thin, too rich, or have too many books.
~ *Carter Burden, Vogue*

Book-love, I say again, lasts throughout life, it never flags or fails, but, like Beauty itself, is a joy forever.
~ *Holbrook Jackson, The Anatomy of Bibliomana Vol.II*

The written word remains. The spoken word takes wing and cannot be recalled.
~ *Anonymous*

An author who speaks about his own books is almost as bad as a mother who talks about her own children.
~ *Benjamin Disraeli*

Be careful about reading health books. You may die of a misprint.
~ *Mark Twain*

Books, like proverbs, receive their chief value from the stamp and esteem of the ages through which they have passed.
~ *J P Getty*

You importune me, Tucca, to present you with my books. I shall not do so; for you want to sell, not to read, them.
~ *Martial*

Hugh Grant and I both laugh and cringe at the same things, worship the same books, eat the same food, hate central heating and sleep with the window open. I thought these things were vital, but being two peas in a pod ended up not being enough.
~ *Liz Hurley*

Books let us into their souls and lay open to us the secrets of our own.
~ *William Hazlitt*

But, indeed, we prefer books to pounds; and we love manuscripts better than florins; and we prefer small pamphlets to war horses.
~ *Isaac Disraeli*

My only books
Were woman's looks,
And folly's all they've taught me.
~ *Thomas Moore*

All of the books in the world contain no more information than is broadcast as video in a single large American city in a single year. Not all bits have equal value.
~ *Carl Sagan*

Books think for me. I can read anything which I call a book.
~ *Charles Lamb*

A morning-glory at my window satisfies me more than the metaphysics of books.
~ *Walt Whitman*

The most accomplished way of using books is to serve them as some people do lords; learn their titles and then brag of their acquaintance.
~ *Laurence Sterne*

I still find each day too short for all the thoughts I want to think, all the walks I want to take, all the books I want to read, and all the friends I want to see.
~ *John Burrough*

Your second-hand bookseller is second to none in the worth of the treasures he dispenses.
~ *Leigh Hunt*

I suggest that the only books that influence us are those for which we are ready, and which have gone a little further down our particular path than we have gone ourselves.
~ *E M Forster*

Censorship ends in logical completeness when nobody is allowed to read any books except the books that nobody reads.
~ *George Bernard Shaw*

There were two things Janey Little loved best in the world: music and books, and not necessarily in that order.
~ *Charles De Lint*

Who knows for what we live, struggle and die?... Wise men write many books, in words too hard to understand. But this, the

purpose of our lives, the end of all our struggle, is beyond all human wisdom.
~ *Alan Paton*

Unlearned men of books assume the care,
As eunuchs are the guardians of the fair
~ *Edward Young*

Unless we change our ways and our direction, our greatness as a nation will soon be a footnote in the history books, a distant memory of an offshore island, lost in the mists of time like Camelot, remembered kindly for its noble past.
~ *Margaret Thatcher*

Obviously there will be a sense of achievement... I suppose there will be some benefits to not writing Harry Potter books any more. So it is about fifty-fifty really.
~ *J K Rowling*

Books are the treasured wealth of the world and the fit inheritance of generations and nations.
~ *Henry David Thoreau*

The proper study of mankind is books (Crome Yellow)
~ *Aldous Huxley*

It is a great thing to start life with a small number of really good books which are your very own.
~ *Sir Arthur Conan Doyle*

We go to school to learn to work hard for money. I write books and create products that teach people how to have money work hard for them.
~ *Robert Kiyosaki*

University printing presses exist, and are subsidised by the Government for the purpose of producing books which no one can read; and they are true to their high calling.
~ *Francis Cornford*

Without books the development of civilization would have been impossible. They are the engines of change, windows on the world, 'Lighthouses' as the poet said 'erected in the sea of time.' They are companions, teachers, magicians, bankers of the treasures of the mind. Books are humanity in print.
~ *Arthur Schopenhauer*

You do know I'm wanting to borrow books, not money or a key to a suite at the Cipriani?
~ *Lucy Mangan*

The impulse to dream was slowly beaten out of me by experience. Now it surged up again and I hungered for books, new ways of looking and seeing.
~ *Richard Wright*

The profit of books is according to the sensibility of the reader. The profoundest thought or passion sleeps as in a mine, until an equal mind and heart finds and publishes it.
~ *Ralph Waldo Emerson*

The best books... are those that tell you what you know already.
~ *George Orwell*

Master books, but do not let them master you. Read to live, not live to read.
~ *Edward Bulwer-Lytton*

If sex is such a natural phenomenon, how come there are so many books on how to do it?
~ *Bette Midler*

It is with books as with women, where a certain plainness of manner and of dress is more engaging than that glare of paint and airs and apparel which may dazzle the eye, but reaches not the affections.
~ *David Hume*

If my books had been any worse, I should not have been invited to Hollywood, and if they had been any better, I should not have come.
~ *Raymond Chandler*

Books are a languid pleasure.
~ *Montaigne*

Go, litel book, go litel myn tragedie.
O moral Gower, this book I directe To thee.
~ *Geoffrey Chaucer*

I have known her pass the whole evening without mentioning a single book, or in fact anything unpleasant at all.
~ *Henry Reed*

The book you don't read can't help.
~ *Jim Rohn*

'Tis pleasant, sure, to see one's name in print;
A book's a book, although there's nothing in't.
~ *Lord Byron*

I keep my books at the British Museum and at Mudie's.
~ *Samuel Butler*

How many a man has dated a new era in his life from the reading of a book.
~ *Henry David Thoreau*

The books one reads in childhood, and perhaps most of all the bad and good bad books, create in one's mind a sort of false map of the world, a series of fabulous countries into which one can retreat at odd moments throughout the rest of life, and which in some cases can even survive a visit to the real countries which they are supposed to represent.
~ *George Orwell*

Books! I dunno if I ever told you this, but books are the greatest gift one person can give another.
~ *Anonymous*

A great book should leave you with many experiences, and slightly exhausted. You should live several lives while reading it.
~ *William Styron*

There can hardly be a stranger commodity in the world than books. Printed by people who don't understand them; sold by people who don't understand them; bound, criticized and read by people who don't understand them; and now even written by people who don't understand them.
~ *Georg Christoph Lichtenberg*

He fed his spirit with the bread of books.
~ *Edwin Markham*

Who kills a man kills a reasonable creature, God's image; but he who destroys a good book, kills reason itself, kills the image of God, as it were in the eye.
~ *John Milton*

Child! do not throw this book about;
Refrain from the unholy pleasure
Of cutting all the pictures out!
Preserve it as your chiefest treasure.
~ *Hilaire Belloc*

From my point of view, a book is a literary prescription put up for the benefit of someone who needs it.
~ *S.M. Crothers*

Bread of flour is good; but there is bread, sweet as honey, if we would eat it, in a good book.
~ *John Ruskin*

A book is a garden, an orchard, a storehouse, a party, a company by the way, a counsellor, a multitude of counsellors.
~ *Henry Ward Beecher*

The multitude of books is making us ignorant.
~ *Voltaire*

Do give books ~ religious or otherwise ~ for Christmas. They're never fattening, seldom sinful, and permanently personal.
~ *Lenore Hershey*

No furniture so charming as books.
~ *Sydney Smith*

I suggest that the only books that influence us are those for which we are ready, and which have gone a little farther down our particular path than we have yet got ourselves.
~ *E.M. Forster*

A house is no home unless it contains food and fire for the mind as well as for the body.
~ *Margaret Fuller*

Never lend books, for no one ever returns them; the only books I have in my library are books that other folks have lent me.
~ *Anatole France*

Just the knowledge that a good book is awaiting one at the end of a long day makes that day happier.
~ *Kathleen Norris*

Book lovers will understand me, and they will know too that part of the pleasure of a library lies in its very existence.
~ *Jan Morris*

Books are the compasses and telescopes and sextants and charts which other men have prepared to help us navigate the dangerous seas of human life.
~ *Anonymous*

Books are the best of things, well used; abused, the worst. What is the right use? What is the end which all means go to effect? They are for nothing but to inspire. I had better never see a book than be warped by its attraction clean out of my own orbit, and made a satelite instead of a system.
~ *Ralph Waldo Emerson*

Good as it is to inherit a library, it is better to collect one.
~ *Augustine Birrell*

Books are the glass of council to dress ourselves by.
~ *Bulstrode Whitlock*

Books are immortal sons deifying their sires.
~ *Plato*

An anthology is like all the plums and orange peel picked out of a cake.
~ *Walter Raleigh*

What is the use of a book,' thought Alice, 'without pictures or conversation?
~ *Lewis Carroll*

Having your book turned into a movie is like seeing your oxen turned into bouillon cubes.
~ *John LeCarre*

Never judge a cover by its book.
~ *Fran Lebowitz*

And further, by these, my son, be admonished: of making many books there is no end; and much study is a weariness of the flesh.
~ *Bible: Ecclesiastes*

Books, we are told, propose to instruct or to amuse. Indeed!…The true antithesis to knowledge, in this case, is not pleasure, but power. All that is literature seeks to communicate power; all that is not literature, to communicate knowledge.
~ *Thomas De Quincey*

These are not books, lumps of lifeless paper, but minds alive on the shelves.
~ *Gilbert Highet*

When I am dead, I hope it may be said:
'His sins were scarlet, but his books were read.
~ *Hilaire Belloc*

The true system of the World has been recognized, developed and perfected...Everything has been discussed and analysed, or at least mentioned.
~ *Jean d'Alembert*

Not with blinded eyesight poring over miserable books.
~ *Alfred, Lord Tennyson*

Borrowers of books ~ those mutilators of collections, spoilers of the symmetry of shelves, and creators of odd volumes.
~ *Charles Lamb*

To read without reflecting is like eating without digesting.
~ *Edmund Burke*

Nothing is worth reading that does not require an alert mind.
~ *Charles Dudley Warner*

The walls of books around him, dense with the past, formed a kind of insulation against the present world and its disasters.
~ *Ross MacDonald*

I've never known any trouble that an hour's reading didn't assuage.
~ *Charles de Secondat*

A good book is always on tap; it may be decanted and drunk a hundred times, and it is still there for further imbibement.
~ *Holbrook Jackson*

The book of the moment often has immense vogue, while the book of the age, which comes in its company from the press, lies unnoticed; but the great book has its revenge. It lives to see its contemporary pushed up shelf by shelf until it finds its final resting-place in the garret or the auction room.
~ *Hamilton Wright Mabie*

In books lies the soul of the whole Past Time: the articulate audible voice of the Past, when the body and material substance of it has altogether vanished like a dream.
~ *Thomas Carlyle*

And you shall sleep restful nights.
~ *Anonymous*

My brother-in-law wrote an unusual murder story. The victim got killed by a man from another book.
~ *Robert Sylvester*

Men of power have not time to read; yet men who do not read are unfit for power.
~ *Michael Foot*

A book lying idle on a shelf is wasted ammunition. Like money, books must be kept in constant circulation. Lend and borrow to the maximum — of both books and money! But especially books, for books represent infinitely more than money. A book is not only a friend, it makes friends for you. When you have possessed a book with mind and spirit, you are enriched. But when you pass it on you are enriched threefold.
~ *Henry Miller*

Books were my pass to personal freedom. I learned to read at age three, and soon discovered there was a whole world to conquer that went beyond our farm in Mississippi.
~ *Oprah Winfrey*

Most books, like their authors, are born to die; of only a few books can it be said that death hath no dominion over them; they live, and their influence lives forever.
~ *J. Swartz*

The pleasure of all reading is doubled when one lives with another who shares the same books.
~ *Katharine Mansfield*

To sit alone in the lamplight with a book spread out before you, and hold intimate converse with men of unseen generations ~ such is a pleasure beyond compare.
~ *Kenko Yoshida*

I'm trying to read a book on how to relax, but I keep falling asleep.
~ *Jim Loy*

No man can be called friendless who has God and the companionship of good books.

~ *Elizabeth Barrett Browning*

There are books so alive that you're always afraid that while you weren't reading, the book has gone and changed, has shifted like a river; while you went on living, it went on living too, and like a river moved on and moved away. No one has stepped twice into the same river. But did anyone ever step twice into the same book?

~ *Marina Tsvetaeva*

Lord! when you sell a man a book you don't sell just twelve ounces of paper and ink and glue ~ you sell him a whole new life. Love and friendship and humour and ships at sea by night ~ there's all heaven and earth in a book, a real book.

~ *Christopher Morley*

There are some books that refuse to be written. They stand their ground year after year and will not be persuaded. It isn't because the book is not there and worth being written — it is only because the right form of the story does not present itself. There is only one right form for a story and if you fail to find that form the story will not tell itself.

~ *Mark Twain*

He felt about books as doctors feel about medicines, or managers about plays ~ cynical but hopeful.

~ *Rose Macaulay*

A man's got to take a lot of punishment to write a really funny book.

~ *Ernest Hemingway*

Let your bookcases and your shelves be your gardens and your pleasure-grounds. Pluck the fruit that grows therein, gather the roses, the spices, and the myrrh.
~ *Judah Ibn Tibbon*

If you resist reading what you disagree with, how will you ever acquire deeper insights into what you believe? The things most worth reading are precisely those that challenge our convictions.
~ *Anonymous*

Master books, but do not let them master you. ~ Read to live, not live to read.
~ *Owen Meredith*

I would never read a book if it were possible for me to talk half an hour with the man who wrote it.
~ *Woodrow Wilson*

As a rule reading fiction is as hard to me as trying to hit a target by hurling feathers at it. I need resistance to celebrate!
~ *William James*

When I can't sleep, I read a book by Steve Allen.
~ *Oscar Levant*

I love to lose myself in other men's minds…. Books think for me.
~ *Charles Lamb*

Anyone who says they have only one life to live must not know how to read a book.
~ *Anonymous*

Books are the quietest and most constant of friends; they are the most accessible and wisest of counselors, and the most patient of teachers.
~ *Charles W. Eliot*

It is what you read when you don't have to that determines what you will be when you can't help it.
~ *Oscar Wilde*

A book is a mirror: if an ape looks into it an apostle is hardly likely to look out.
~ *Georg C. Lichtenberg*

It is chiefly through books that we enjoy the intercourse with superior minds... In the best books, great men talk to us, give us their most previous thought, and pour their souls into ours. God be thanked for books.
~ *William Ellery Channing*

Read the best books first, or you may not have a chance to read them all.
~ *Henry David Thoreau*

A well-composed book is a magic carpet on which we are wafted to a world that we cannot enter in any other way.
~ *Caroline Gordon*

The test of literature is, I suppose, whether we ourselves live more intensely for the reading of it.
~ *Elizabeth Drew*

Readers are plentiful, thinkers are rare.
~ *Harriet Martineau*

Books are delightful society. If you go into a room and find it full
of books ~ even without taking them from the shelves they seem
to speak to you, to bid you welcome.
~ *William Ewart Gladstone*

God be thanked for books! they are the voices of the distant and
the dead, and make us heirs of the spiritual life of past ages.
~ *W.E. Channing*

To every man who struggles with his own soul in mystery, a book
that is a book flowers once, and seeds, and is gone.
~ *D. H. Lawrence*

The man who does not read good books has no advantage over
the man who can't read them.
~ *Mark Twain*

When you reread a classic you do not see more in the book than
you did before; you see more in you than was there before.
~ *Clifton Fadiman*

How long most people would look at the best book before they
would give the price of a large turbot for it!
~ *John Ruskin*

Good friends, good books and a sleepy conscience: this is the
ideal life.
~ *Mark Twain*

My test of a good novel is dreading to begin the last chapter.
~ *Thomas Helm*

To read a book for the first time is to make an acquaintance with a new friend; to read it for a second time is to meet an old one.
~ *Chinese Proverb*

For books are more than books, they are the life
The very heart and core of ages past,
The reason why men lived and worked and died,
The essence and quintessence of their lives.
~ *Amy Lowell*

For friends... do but look upon good Books: they are true friends, that will neither flatter nor dissemble.
~ *Sir Francis Bacon*

Always read something that will make you look good if you die in the middle of it.
~ *P.J. O'Rourke*

The wise man reads both books and life itself.
~ *Lin Yutang*

He that loveth a book will never want for a faithful friend, a wholesome counselor, a cheerful companion, an effectual comforter.
~ *Isaac Barrow*

In the middle of the silence in a writer's house lies an invalid: the book being worked on.
~ *Richard Eder*

I am like a book, with pages that have stuck together for want of use: my mind needs unpacking and the truths stored within must be turned over from time to time, to be ready when occasion demands.
~ *Seneca*

Due attention to the inside of books, and due contempt for the outside, is the proper relation between a man of sense and his books.
~ *Earl of Chesterfield*

All books are either dreams or swords,
You can cut, or you can drug, with words.
~ *Amy Lowell*

Books are embalmed minds.
~ *Bovee*

People get nothing out of books but what they bring to them.
~ *George Bernard Shaw*

Books can be dangerous. The best ones should be labeled This could change your life.
~ *Helen Exley*

I have a real soft spot in my heart for librarians and people who care about books.
~ *Ann Richards*

A book is to me like a hat or coat ~ a very uncomfortable thing until the newness has been worn off.
~ *Charles B. Fairbanks*

To choose a good book, look in an inquisitor's prohibited list.
~ *John Aikin*

Reading means borrowing.
~ *Georg Christoph Lichtenberg*

The worth of a book is to be measured by what you can carry away from it.
~ *James Bryce*

Only your friends steal your books.
~ *Voltaire*

Books, I don't know what you see in them…I can understand a person reading them, but I can't for the life of me see why people have to write them.
~ *Peter Ustinov*

A dirty book is rarely dusty.
~ *Anonymous*

Few books today are forgivable.
~ *R. D. Laing*

He who lends a book is an idiot. He who returns the book is more of an idiot.
~ *Arabic Proverb*

Get stewed: Books are a load of crap.
~ *Philip Larkin*

There is a great deal of difference between an eager man who wants to read a book and a tired man who wants a book to read.
~ *G.K. Chesterton*

A book is the only place in which you can examine a fragile thought without breaking it, or explore an explosive idea without fear it will go off in your face. It is one of the few havens remaining where a man's mind can get both provocation and privacy.
~ *Edward P. Morgan*

A best-seller is the gilded tomb of a mediocre talent.
~ *Logan Pearsall Smith*

The books that help you most are those which make you think the most. The hardest way of learning is that of easy reading; but a great book that comes from a great thinker is a ship of thought, deep freighted with truth and beauty.
~ *Theodore Parker*

This is not a novel to be tossed aside lightly. It should be thrown with great force.
~ *Dorothy Parker*

A wonderful thing about a book, in contrast to a computer screen, is that you can take it to bed with you.
~ *Daniel J. Boorstein*

Books must follow sciences, and not sciences books.
~ *Sir Francis Bacon*

A book is like a garden carried in the pocket.
~ *Chinese Proverb*

It is all very well to be able to write books, but can you waggle your ears?
~ *J. M. Barrie*

My Book and Heart Must never part.
~ *Anonymous*

Lawyer without books would be like a workman without tools.
~ *Thomas Jefferson*

I find television to be very educating. Every time somebody turns on the set, I go in the other room and read a book.
~ *Groucho Marx*

Books ~ the best antidote against the marsh-gas of boredom and vacuity.
~ *George Steiner*

Books are the bees which carry the quickening pollen from one to another mind.
~ *James Russell Lowell*

Books cannot always please, however good;
Minds are not ever craving for their food.
~ *George Crabbe*

Books and friends should be few but good.
~ *Proverb*

A good book is the best of friends, the same to-day and forever.
~ *Martin Tupper*

All books are divisible into two classes, the books of the hour, and the books of all time.
~ *John Ruskin*

At last, an unprintable book that is readable.
~ *Ezra Pound*

Books are for people who wish they were somewhere else.
~ *Mark Twain*

A book is not harmless merely because no one is consciously offended by it.
~ *T. S. Eliot*

There is no such thing as a moral or an immoral book. Books are well written, or badly written.
~ *Oscar Wilde*

Be careful about reading health books. You may die of a misprint.
~ *Mark Twain*

A book may be amusing with numerous errors, or it may be very dull without a single absurdity.
~ *Oliver Goldsmith*

A book is a gift you can open again and again.
~ *Garrison Keillor*

If a book is really good, it deserves to be read again, and if it's great, it should be read at least three times.
~ *Anatole Broyard*

We all know that books burn ~ yet we have the greater knowledge that books cannot be killed by fire. People die, but books never die. No man and no force can abolish memory... In this war, we know, books are weapons.
~ *Franklin D. Roosevelt*

If a book is worth reading, it is worth buying.
~ *John Ruskin*

A best-seller was a book which somehow sold well simply because it was selling well.
~ *Daniel J. Boorstin*

A good book on your shelf is a friend that turns its back on you and remains a friend.
~ *Anonymous*

We shouldn't teach great books; we should teach a love of reading.
~ *B. F. Skinner*

When a new book is published, read an old one.
~ *Samuel Rogers*

A good book should leave you... slightly exhausted at the end. You live several lives while reading it.
~ *William Styron*

Americans like fat books and thin women.
~ *Russell Baker*

Books serve to show a man that those original thoughts of his aren't very new after all.
~ *Abraham Lincoln*

A good book has no ending.
~ *R.D. Cumming*

A classic is a book which people praise and don't read.
~ *Mark Twain*

In recommending a book to a friend the less said the better. The moment you praise a book too highly you awaken resistance in your listener.
~ *Henry Miller*

When I can't sleep, I read a book by Steve Allen.
~ *Oscar Levant*

I was going to buy a copy of The Power of Positive Thinking, and then I thought: What the hell good would that do?
~ *Ronnie Shakes*

I just got out of the hospital. I was in a speed-reading accident. I hit a bookmark.
~ *Steven Wright*

I have only ever read one book in my life, and that is White Fang. It's so frightfully good I've never bothered to read another.
~ *Nancy Mitford (Love in a Cold Climate, 1949)*

I'm trying to read a book on how to relax, but I keep falling asleep.
~ *Jim Loy*

A man's got to take a lot of punishment to write a really funny book.
~ *Ernest Hemingway*

Once you've put one of his books down, you simply can't pick it up again.
~ *Mark Twain (talking about Henry James)*

A book is like a garden carried in the pocket.
~ Chinese Proverb

We shouldn't teach great books; we should teach a love of reading.
~ *B. F. Skinner*

Books like friends, should be few and well-chosen.
~ *Samuel Johnson*

A lawyer without books would be like a workman without tools.
~ *Thomas Jefferson*

Books are humanity in spirit.
~ *Barbara W. Tuchman*

Of writing many books there is no end.
~ *Elizabeth Barrett Browning*

It is what you read when you don't have to that determines what you will be when you can't help it.
~ *Oscar Wilde*

For friends... do but look upon good Books: they are true friends, that will neither flatter nor dissemble.
~ *Sir Francis Bacon*

She is too fond of books, and it has turned her brain.
~ *Louisa May Alcott*

All books are divisible into two classes, the books of the hours and the books of all times.
~ *James Ruskin*

'What is the use of a book,' thought Alice, 'without pictures or conversations?'
~ *Lewis Carroll (Alice's Adventures in Wonderland, 1865)*

A truly great books should be read in youth, again in maturity and once more in old age, as a fine building should be seen by morning light, at noon and by moonlight.
~ *Robertson Davies (In Grant, The Enthusiasms of Robertson Davies)*

The reading of all good books is like a conversation with the finest men of past centuries.
~ *Rene Descartes (Discours de la Methode, 1637)*

The book is the world's most patient medium.
~ *Northrop Frye (The Scholar in Society, Film, 1984)*

For a true writer each book should be a new beginning, where he tries again for something that is beyond attainment.
~ *Ernest Hemingway (Speech for the presentation of the Nobel Prize-1954)*

A book is like a piece of rope; it takes on meaning only in connection with the things it holds together.
~ *Norman Cousins*

When you read to a child, when you put a book in a child's hands, you are bringing that child news of the infinitely varied nature of life. You are an awakener.
~ *Paula Fox*

There are no bad books any more than there are ugly women.
~ *Anatole France*

When you re read a classic you do not see more in the book than you did before; you see more in you than there was before.
~ *Thomas Carlyle*

A book, tight shut, is but a block of paper.
~ *Chinese Proverb*

A good book is the precious life blood of a master spirit, embalmed and treasured up on purpose to a life beyond life.
~ *John Milton*

Books are more than books. They are the life, the very heart and core of ages past, the reason why men lived and worded and died, the essence and quintessence of their lives.
~ *Amy Lowell*

If I read a book that impresses me, I have to take myself firmly by the hand, before I mix with other people; otherwise they would think my mind rather queer.
~ *Anne Frank*

What is the use of a book, thought Alice, without pictures or conversations!
~ *Lewis Caroll, Alice's Adventures in Wonderland*

If you are going to get anywhere in life you have to read a lot of books.
~ *Roald Dahl*

A man is known by the books he reads.
~ *Ralph Waldo Emerson*

No two persons ever read the same book.
~ *Edmund Wilson*

All modern American literature comes from one book by Mark Twain called Huckleberry Finn. American writing comes from that. There was nothing before. There has been nothing as good since.
~ *Ernest Hemingway*

Books do furnish a room.
~ *Anthony Powell*

It is often said that one has but one life to live, but that is nonsense. For one who reads, there is no limit to the number of lives that may be lived, for fiction, biography, and history offer an inexhaustible number of lives in all periods of time.
~ *Louis L'Amour*

He had been so busy getting away from the library, he hadn't paid attention to where he was going.
~ *J.K. Rowling*

A book must be the axe for the frozen sea inside us.
~ *Franz Kafka*

A book that [is] fitly chosen is a life-long friend.
~ *Douglas Jerrold*

I like to read because it's the opposite of being on the go. Reading is the perfect antidote.
~ *Joe Strummer*

As long as I'm reading, I'm at home.
~ *George Foreman*

Books are the quietest and most constant of friends; they are the most accessible and wisest of counsellors, and the most patient of teachers.
~ *Charles W. Eliot, The Happy Life*

Books are the quietest and most constant of friends: they are the most accessible and wisest of counselors, and the most patient of teachers.
~ *Charles W. Eliot*

I love a garden and a book.
~ *Eliza Lucas Pinckney*

We will always return to the private and inviolable act of reading as our culture's way of developing an individual.
~ *Guy Davenport*

Books have a life of their own.
~ *Latin Proverb*

There is more treasure in books than in all the pirates' loot on Treasure Island... and the best of all, you can enjoy these riches every day of your life.
~ *Walt Disney*

I read books like mad, but I am careful to to let anything I read influence me.
~ *Michael Caine*

A book is the only place in which you can examine a fragile thought without breaking it.
~ *Edward P. Morgan*

People die, but books never die. No man and no force can abolish memory.
~ *Franklin D. Roosevelt*

Read not to contradict and confute, nor to believe and take for granted, nor to find talk and discourse, but to weigh and consider.
~ *Sir Francis Bacon*

When you read with your child, you show them that reading is important, but you also show them they're important — that they are so important to you that you will spend 20 minutes a day with your arm around them.
~ *Laura Bush, 9/03*

Books do not make life easier or more simple, but harder and more interesting.
~ *Harry Golden*

If you cannot read all your books, at any rate handle, or as it were, fondle them ~ peer into them, let them fall open where they will, read from the first sentence that arrests the eye, set them back on the shelves with your own hands, arrange them on your own plan so that you at least know where they are. Let them be your friends; let them at any rate be your acquaintances.
~ *Winston Churchill*

The art of reading is in great part that of acquiring a better understanding of life from one's encounter with it in a book.
~ *Andre Maurois*

The instruction we find in books is like fire. We fetch it from our neighbors, kindle it at home, communicate it to others, and it becomes the property of all.

~ *Voltaire*

Above all, a book is a riverbank for the river of language. Language without the riverbank is only television talk — a free fall, a loose splash, a spill.

~ *Cynthia Ozick, Portrait of the Artist as a Bad Character*

Every book that anyone sets out on is a voyage of discovery that may discover nothing. Any voyager may be lost at sea, like John Cabot. Nobody can teach the geography of the undiscovered.

~ *Wallace Stegner*

Comic books are what novels used to be ~ an accessible, vernacular form with mass appeal ~ and if the highbrows are right, they're a form perfectly suited to our dumbed-down culture and collective attention deficit.

~ *Charles McGrath, NY Times, 7/11/04*

Books are the carriers of civilization. Without books, history is silent, literature dumb, science crippled, thought and speculation at a standstill. They are engines of change, windows on the world, lighthouses erected in the sea of time.

~ *Barbara W. Tuchman*

Reading has always been life unwrapped to me, a way of understanding the world and understanding myself through both the unknown and the everyday. If being a parent consists often of passing along chunks of ourselves to unwitting often unwilling, recipients, then books are, for me, one of the simplest and most sure-fire ways of doing that.

~ *Anna Quindlen*

Reading without reflection is like eating without digesting.
~ *Edmund Burke*

Read, Read, and then Read some more. Always Read. Find the voices that speak most to YOU. This is your pleasure and blessing, as well as responsibility!
~ *Naomi Shihab Nye*

A good book is the best of friends, the same today and forever.
~ *Martin Tupper*

Bad books are about things the writer already knew before he wrote them.
~ *Carlos Fuentes*

All books are either dreams or swords. You can cut or you can drug with words.
~ *Amy Lowell*

I have never known any trouble that an hour's reading didn't assuage.
~ *Montesquieu*

Literature is my Utopia. Here I am not disenfranchised. No barrier of the senses shuts me out from the sweet, gracious discourses of my book friends. They talk to me without embarrassment or awkwardness.
~ *Helen Keller*

You think your pains and heartbreaks are unprecedented in the history of the world, but then you read. It was books that taught me that the things that tormented me were the very things that connected me with all the people who were alive, or who have ever been alive.
~ *James Baldwin*

I think reading is a lyric writer's best secret weapon.
~ *Jason Blume, Secrets of Songwriting (2003)*

There are few sights sadder than a ruined book.
~ *Lemony Snicket, Wide Window*

Reading~ not occasionally, not only on vacation but everyday~ gives me nourishment and enlarges my life in mysterious and essential ways.
~ *Mona Simpson, O, 5/01*

Good books are the warehouses of ideas.
~ *H. G. Wells*

From candlelight to early bedtime, I read.
~ *Thomas Jefferson*

We are all writers and readers as well as communicators with the need at times to please and satisfy ourselves with the clear and almost perfect thought.
~ *Roger Angell*

To sit alone in the lamplight with a book spread out before you, and hold intimate converse with men of unseen generations ~ such is a pleasure beyond compare.
~ *Kenko Yoshida*

Traversing a slow page, to come upon a lode of the pure shining metal is to exult inwardly for greedy hours.
~ *Kathleen Norris*

Before entering the seminary, I had not encountered the life-changing potential of reading as a source of meaning, as a way of ordering one's inner life, and being rooted in the world.
~ *James Carroll*

People who are passionate about reading do not have to be convinced of its benefits... We turn to books when we are lonely or when other people overwhelm us. Books are there for us whether we're celebrating or in mourning.
~ *Elisabeth Ellington/Jane Freimiller, A Year of Reading*

A good book should leave you ... slightly exhausted at the end. You live several lives while reading it.
~ *William Styron*

The big advantage of a book is that it's very easy to rewind. Close it and you're right back at the beginning.
~ *Jerry Seinfeld*

A book is not only a friend, it makes friends for you. When you have possessed a book with mind and spirit, you are enriched. But when you pass it on you are enriched threefold.
~ *Henry Miller*

E heluhelu kakou. (Let's read together.)
A book ought to be an ice pick to break up the frozen sea within us.
~ *Franz Kafka*

A good book is the best of friends, the same today and forever.
~ *Martin Tupper*

A good book is the precious lifeblood of a master spirit.
~ *John Milton*

A truly great book should be read in youth, once again in maturity and once more in old age, as a fine building should be seen by morning light, at noon and by moonlight.
~ *Robertson Davies*

The reading of all good books is like a conversation with the finest minds of past centuries.
~ *Rene Descartes*

When you give someone a book, you don't give him just paper, ink, and glue. You give him the possibility of a whole new life.
~ *Christopher Morley*

Certain books come to meet me, as do people.
~ *Elizabeth Bowen*

There are many little ways to enlarge your child's world. Love of books is the best of all.
~ *Jacqueline Kennedy Onassis*

I used to read every, well, most nights. I think reading helps me in terms of relaxing... It helps me to get my mind off the game a little bit more and it helps me to be a little bit more focused.
~ *Rio Ferdinand*

Read. Read every chance you get. Read to keep growing. Read history. Read poetry. Read for pure enjoyment. Read a book called Life on a Little Known Planet. It's about insects. It will make you feel better.
~ *David McCullough, Dartmouth, 2003*

Books are meat and medicine and flame and flight and flower steel, stitch, cloud and clout, and drumbeats on the air.
~ *Gwendolyn Brooks*

In reading, one should notice and fondle details.
~ *Vladimir Nabokov*

Reading books removes sorrows from the heart.
~ *Moroccan Proverb*

There is no shortage of wonderful writers. What we lack is a dependable mass of readers.
~ *Kurt Vonnegut, Jr.. The Independent, 1977*

The greatest gift is a passion for reading. It is cheap, it consoles, it distracts, it excites, it gives you knowledge of the world and experience of a wide kind. It is a moral illumination.
~ *Elizabeth Hardwick*

What is reading but a silent conversation?
~ *Walter Savage Landor*

Books are the quietest and most constant of friends, and the most patient of teachers.
~ *Charles W. Eliot*

I have an intimate relationship with books. After all, I take them with me into the bathtub—not an invitation I offer lightly.
~ *Gina Barreca, The Book that Changed My Life*

I believe in the absolute and unlimited liberty of reading. I believe in wandering through the stacks and picking out the first thing that strikes me. I believe in choosing books based on the dust jacket.
~ *Rick Moody, This I Believe*

Sometimes when I think how good my book can be, I can hardly breathe.
~ *Truman Capote*

Books are Y2K compliant.
~ *Unknown*

The book to read is not the one which thinks for you, but the one which makes you think.
~ *James McCosh*

He who destroys a good book kills reason itself.
~ *John Milton*

Be as careful of the books you read, as of the company you keep, for your habits and character will be as much influenced by the former as the latter.
~ *Paxton Hood*

Don't join the book burners... Don't be afraid to go in your library and read every book.
~ *Dwight D. Eisenhower*

Except a living man, there is nothing more wonderful than a book.
~ *Charles Kingsley*

A good word is like a good tree whose root is firmly fixed and whose top is in the sky.
~ *The Koran*

What's a book?
Everything or nothing.
The eye that sees it all.
~ *Ralph Waldo Emerson*

Wherever they burn books they will also, in the end, burn human beings.
~ *Heinrich Heine*

Books are the quietest and most constant of friends: they are the most accessible and wisest of counsellors, and the most patient of teachers.
~ *Charles W. Eliot*

Reading is to the mind what exercise is to the body.
~ *Richard Steele*

Force yourself to reflect on what you read, paragraph by paragraph.
~ *Samuel Taylor Coleridge*

I had just taken to reading. I had just discovered the art of leaving my body to sit impassive in a crumpled up attitude in a chair or sofa, while I wandered over the hills and far away in novel company and new scenes... My world began to expand very rapidly,... the reading habit had got me securely.
~ *H. G. Wells*

I have often reflected upon the new vistas that reading opened to me. I knew right there in prison that reading had changed forever the course of my life. As I see it today, the ability to read awoke in me some long dormant craving to be mentally alive.
~ *Malcolm X*

In a very real sense, people who have read good literature have lived more than people who cannot or will not read.
~ *S. I. Hayakawa*

It is no more necessary that a man should remember the different dinners and suppers which have made him healthy, than the different books which have made him wise. Let us see the results of good food in a strong body, and the results of great reading in a full and powerful mind.
~ *Sydney Smith*

Let us read with method, and propose to ourselves an end to which our studies may point. The use of reading is to aid us in thinking.
~ *Edward Gibbon*

The more that you read,
the more things you will know.
The more that you learn,
the more places you'll go.
~ *Dr. Seuss*

Resolve to edge in a little reading every day, if it is but a single sentence. If you gain fifteen minutes a day, it will make itself felt at the end of the year.
~ *Horace Mann*

Readers may be divided into four classes:
I. Sponges, who absorb all that they read and return it in nearly the same state, only a little dirtied.
II. Sand-glasses, who retain nothing and are content to get through a book for the sake of getting through the time.
III. Strain-bags, who retain merely the dregs of what they read.
IV. Mogul diamonds, equally rare and valuable, who profit by what they read, and enable others to profit by it also.
~ *Samuel Taylor Coleridge*

The best effect of any book is that it excites the reader to self activity.
~ *Thomas Carlyle*

The way a book is read ~ which is to say, the qualities a reader brings to a book ~ can have as much to do with its worth as anything the author puts into it.
~ *Norman Cousins*

Fiction is like a spider's web, attached ever so lightly perhaps, but still attached to life at all four corners.
~ *Virginia Woolf*

My mother and my father were illiterate immigrants from Russia. When I was a child they were constantly amazed that I could go to a building and take a book on any subject. They couldn't believe this access to knowledge we have here in America. They couldn't believe that it was free.
~ *Kirk Douglas*

T'is the good reader that makes the good book.
~ *Ralph Waldo Emerson*

To acquire the habit of reading is to construct for yourself a refuge from almost all the miseries of life.
~ *W. Somerset Maugham*

The end of reading is not more books but more life.
~ *Holbrook Jackson*

Prefer knowledge to wealth, for the one is transitory, the other perpetual.
~ *Socrates*

Literature is my Utopia.
~ *Helen Keller*

Reading maketh a full man.
~ *Sir Francis Bacon*

When I got [my] library card, that was when my life began.
~ *Rita Mae Brown*

In a library we are surrounded by many hundreds of dear friends imprisoned by an enchanter in paper and leathern boxes.
~ *Ralph Waldo Emerson*

When I... discovered libraries, it was like having Christmas every day.
~ *Jean Fritz*

Words are the voice of the heart.
~ *Confucius*

We read to know we are not alone.
~ *C.S. Lewis*

The love of learning, the sequestered nooks, and all the sweet serenity of books.
~ *Henry Wadsworth Longfellow (1807 - 1882)*

Some books are to be tasted, others to be swallowed, and some few to be chewed and digested: that is, some books are to be read only in parts, others to be read, but not curiously, and some few to be read wholly, and with diligence and attention.
~ *Sir Sir Francis Bacon (1561 - 1626)*

An investment in knowledge always pays the best interest.
~ *Benjamin Franklin*

> I've traveled the world twice over,
> Met the famous; saints and sinners,
> Poets and artists, kings and queens,
> Old stars and hopeful beginners,
> I've been where no-one's been before,
> Learned secrets from writers and cooks
> All with one library ticket
> To the wonderful world of books.
> ~ *Unknown*

Knowledge is knowing... or knowing where to find out.
~ *Alvin Toffler*

None is poor save him that lacks knowledge.
~ *The Talmud*

Learning is weightless, a treasure you can always carry easily.
~ *Chinese Proverb*

Read not to contradict and confute, nor to find talk and discourse, but to weigh and consider.
~ *Sir Sir Francis Bacon (1561 - 1626)*

I aimed at the public's heart, and by accident I hit it in the stomach.
~ *Upton Sinclair (1878 - 1968), on his novel, The Jungle (1906)*

Oh for a book and a shady nook...
~ *John Wilson (1785 - 1854)*

When I read a book I seem to read it with my eyes only, but now and then I come across a passage, perhaps only a phrase, which has a meaning for me, and it becomes part of me.
~ *W. Somerset Maugham (1874 - 1965), 'Of Human Bondage', 1915*

Learn as much by writing as by reading.
~ *Lord Acton*

Knowing I lov'd my books, he furnish'd me
From mine own library with volumes that
I prize above my dukedom.
~ *William Shakespeare (1564 - 1616), The Tempest*

Resolve to edge in a little reading every day, if it is but a single sentence. If you gain fifteen minutes a day, it will make itself felt at the end of the year.
~ *Horace Mann (1796 - 1859)*

Never read a book through merely because you have begun it.
~ *John Witherspoon (1723 - 1794)*

Do give books ~ religious or otherwise ~ for Christmas. They're never fattening, seldom sinful, and permanently personal.
~ *Lenore Hershey*

The man who doesn't read good books has no advantage over the man who can't read them.
~ *Mark Twain (1835 - 1910)*

Reading this book is like waiting for the first shoe to drop.
~ *Ralph Novak*

When I am attacked by gloomy thoughts, nothing helps me so much as running to my books. They quickly absorb me and banish the clouds from my mind.
~ *Michel de Montaigne (1533 - 1592)*

Thank you for sending me a copy of your book. I'll waste no time reading it.
~ *Moses Hadas (1900 - 1966)*

There is no such thing as a moral or an immoral book. Books are well written or badly written.
~ *Oscar Wilde (1854 - 1900), The Picture of Dorian Gray, 1891*

Always read stuff that will make you look good if you die in the middle of it.
~ *P. J. O'Rourke (1947 - )*

In the highest civilization, the book is still the highest delight. He who has once known its satisfactions is provided with a resource against calamity.

~ *Ralph Waldo Emerson (1803 - 1882), Letters and Social Aims*

A truly great book should be read in youth, again in maturity and once more in old age, as a fine building should be seen by morning light, at noon and by moonlight.

~ *Robertson Davies*

To be a book-collector is to combine the worst characteristics of a dope fiend with those of a miser.

~ *Robertson Davies, The Table Talk of Samuel Marchbanks*

Reading is sometimes an ingenious device for avoiding thought.

~ *Sir Arthur Helps*

Reading, after a certain age, diverts the mind too much from its creative pursuits. Any man who reads too much and uses his own brain too little falls into lazy habits of thinking.

~ *Albert Einstein (1879 - 1955)*

This paperback is very interesting, but I find it will never replace a hardcover book ~ it makes a very poor doorstop.

~ *Alfred Hitchcock (1899 - 1980)*

Many books require no thought from those who read them, and for a very simple reason; they made no such demand upon those who wrote them.

~ *Charles Caleb Colton (1780 - 1832), Lacon, 1820*

You can cover a great deal of country in books.
~ *Andrew Lang (1844 - 1912)*

There's a certain kind of conversation you have from time to time at parties in New York about a new book. The word banal sometimes rears its by-now banal head; you say underedited, I say derivative. The conversation goes around and around various literary criticisms, and by the time it moves on one thing is clear: No one read the book; we just read the reviews.
~ *Anna Quindlen (1953 - )*

There is no mistaking a real book when one meets it. It is like falling in love.
~ *Christopher Morley (1890 - 1957)*

> Books to the ceiling,
> Books to the sky,
> My pile of books is a mile high.
> How I love them! How I need them!
> I'll have a long beard by the time I read them.
> ~ *Arnold Lobel*

Wear the old coat and buy the new book.
~ *Austin Phelps*

It was a book to kill time for those who like it better dead.
~ *Dame Rose Macaulay (1881 - 1958)*

Books...are like lobster shells, we surround ourselves with 'em, then we grow out of 'em and leave 'em behind, as evidence of our earlier stages of development.
~ *Dorothy L. Sayers (1893 - 1957), The Unpleasantness at the Bellona Club, 1928*

A good novel tells us the truth about its hero; but a bad novel tells us the truth about its author.
~ *G. K. Chesterton (1874 - 1936)*

Don't join the book burners. Don't think you're going to conceal faults by concealing evidence that they ever existed. Don't be afraid to go in your library and read every book...
~ *Dwight D. Eisenhower (1890 - 1969)*

Most new books are forgotten within a year, especially by those who borrow them.
~ *Evan Esar (1899 - 1995)*

I think it is good that books still exist, but they do make me sleepy.
~ *Frank Zappa (1940 - 1993)*

There is a great deal of difference between an eager man who wants to read a book and the tired man who wants a book to read.
~ *G. K. Chesterton (1874 - 1936)*

Woe be to him that reads but one book.
~ *George Herbert (1593 - 1633)*

I find television very educating. Every time somebody turns on the set, I go into the other room and read a book.
~ *Groucho Marx (1890 - 1977)*

From the moment I picked up your book until I laid it down, I was convulsed with laughter. Some day I intend reading it.
~ *Groucho Marx (1890 - 1977)*

Reading well is one of the great pleasures that solitude can afford
you.
~ *Harold Bloom (1930 - ), O Magazine, April 2003*

The experience of the race shows that we get our most important
education not through books but through our work. We are
developed by our daily task, or else demoralized by it, as by
nothing else.
~ *Anna Garlin Spencer*

I don't think one can accurately measure the historical
effectiveness of a poem; but one does know, of course, that
books influence individuals; and individuals, although they are
part of large economic and social processes, influence history.
Every mass is after all made up of millions of individuals.
~ *Denise Levertov*

I have every sympathy with the American who was so horrified
by what he had read about the effects of smoking that he gave up
reading.
~ *Henry G. Strauss*

If you never ask yourself any questions about the meaning of a
passage, you cannot expect the book to give you any insight you
do not already possess.
~ *Mortimer Adler*

Our house was a temple to The Book. We owned thousands, nay
millions of books. They lined the walls, filled the cupboards, and
turned the floor into a maze far more complex than Hampton
Court's. Books ruled our lives. They were our demigods.
~ *Nick Bantock*

There are some books that refuse to be written. They stand their ground year after year and will not be persuaded. It isn't because the book is not there and worth being written ~ it is only because the right form of the story does not present itself. There is only one right form for a story and if you fail to find that form the story will not tell itself.
~ *Mark Twain*

The difference between literature and journalism is that journalism is unreadable and literature is not read.
~ *Oscar Wilde*

Books are the best of things, well used; abused, the worst. What is the right use? What is the end which all means go to effect? They are for nothing but to inspire. I had better never see a book than be warped by its attraction clean out of my own orbit, and made a satellite instead of a system.
~ *Ralph Waldo Emerson*

Only one hour in a day is more pleasurable than the hour spent in bed with a book before going to sleep, and that is the hour spent in bed with a book after being called in the morning.
~ *Rose Macaulay*

The books which help you most are those which make you think the most. The hardest way of learning is by easy reading: but a great book that comes from a great thinker ~ it is a ship of thought, deep freighted with truth and with beauty.
~ *Theodore Parker*

It is chiefly through books that we enjoy the intercourse with superior minds... In the best books, great men talk to us, give us their most previous thought, and pour their souls into ours. God be thanked for books.
~ *William Ellery Channing*

A book is the only place in which you can examine a fragile thought without breaking it, or explore an explosive idea without fear it will go off in your face. It is one of the few havens remaining where a man's mind can get both provocation and privacy.
~ *Edward P. Morgan*

A good book should leave you... slightly exhausted at the end. You live several lives while reading it.
~ *William Styron, interview, Writers at Work, 1958*

Many people, other than the authors, contribute to the making of a book, from the first person who had the bright idea of alphabetic writing through the inventor of movable type to the lumberjacks who felled the trees that were pulped for its printing. It is not customary to acknowledge the trees themselves, though their commitment is total.
~ *Forsyth and Rada, Machine Learning*

If there's a book you really want to read but it hasn't been written yet, then you must write it.
~ *Toni Morrison*

I find television to be very educating. Every time somebody turns on the set, I go in the other room and read a book.
~ *Groucho Marx*

A book reads the better which is our own, and has been so long known to us, that we know the topography of its blots, and dog's ears, and can trace the dirt in it to having read it at tea with buttered muffins.
~ *Charles Lamb, Last Essays of Elia, 1833*

There's nothing to match curling up with a good book when there's a repair job to be done around the house.
~ *Joe Ryan*

As a rule reading fiction is as hard to me as trying to hit a target by hurling feathers at it. I need resistance to celebrate!
~ *William James*

You know you've read a good book when you turn the last page and feel a little as if you have lost a friend.
~ *Paul Sweeney*

Lord! when you sell a man a book you don't sell just twelve ounces of paper and ink and glue ~ you sell him a whole new life. Love and friendship and humour and ships at sea by night ~ there's all heaven and earth in a book, a real book.
~ *Christopher Morley*

Books serve to show a man that those original thoughts of his aren't very new after all.
~ *Abraham Lincoln*

I've never known any trouble that an hour's reading didn't assuage.
~ *Charles de Secondat, Baron de la Brède et de Montesquieu,*

Fiction reveals truths that reality obscures.
~ *Jessamyn West*

TV. If kids are entertained by two letters, imagine the fun they'll have with twenty-six. Open your child's imagination. Open a book.
~ *Author Unknown*

In reading, a lonely quiet concert is given to our minds; all our mental faculties will be present in this symphonic exaltation.
~ *Stéphane Mallarmé*

Books can be dangerous. The best ones should be labeled This could change your life.
~ *Helen Exley*

There is a wonder in reading Braille that the sighted will never know: to touch words and have them touch you back.
~ *Jim Fiebig*

Good friends, good books and a sleepy conscience: this is the ideal life.
~ *Mark Twain*

If you resist reading what you disagree with, how will you ever acquire deeper insights into what you believe? The things most worth reading are precisely those that challenge our convictions.
~ *Author Unknown*

Until I feared I would lose it, I never loved to read. One does not love breathing.
~ *Harper Lee*

The scholar only knows how dear these silent, yet eloquent, companions of pure thoughts and innocent hours become in the season of adversity. When all that is worldly turns to dross around us, these only retain their steady value.

~ *Washington Irving*

For friends... do but look upon good Books: they are true friends, that will neither flatter nor dissemble.

~ *Sir Francis Bacon*

There are books so alive that you're always afraid that while you weren't reading, the book has gone and changed, has shifted like a river; while you went on living, it went on living too, and like a river moved on and moved away. No one has stepped twice into the same river. But did anyone ever step twice into the same book?

~ *Marina Tsvetaeva*

Medicine for the soul.

~ *Inscription over the door of the Library at Thebes*

The stories of childhood leave an indelible impression, and their author always has a niche in the temple of memory from which the image is never cast out to be thrown on the rubbish heap of things that are outgrown and outlived.

~ *Howard Pyle*

These are not books, lumps of lifeless paper, but minds alive on the shelves. From each of them goes out its own voice... and just as the touch of a button on our set will fill the room with music, so by taking down one of these volumes and opening it, one can call into range the voice of a man far distant in time and space, and hear him speaking to us, mind to mind, heart to heart.

~ *Gilbert Highet*

Children don't read to find their identity, to free themselves from guilt, to quench the thirst for rebellion or to get rid of alienation. They have no use for psychology.... They still believe in God, the family, angels, devils, witches, goblins, logic, clarity, punctuation, and other such obsolete stuff.... When a book is boring, they yawn openly. They don't expect their writer to redeem humanity, but leave to adults such childish illusions.
~ *Isaac Bashevis Singer*

There is a temperate zone in the mind, between luxurious indolence and exacting work; and it is to this region, just between laziness and labor, that summer reading belongs.
~ *Henry Ward Beecher*

If you have never said Excuse me to a parking meter or bashed your shins on a fireplug, you are probably wasting too much valuable reading time.
~ *Sherri Chasin Calvo*

I love to lose myself in other men's minds.... Books think for me.
~ *Charles Lamb*

Far more seemly were it for thee to have thy study full of books, than thy purse full of money.
~ *John Lyly*

I often derive a peculiar satisfaction in conversing with the ancient and modern dead, ~ who yet live and speak excellently in their works. My neighbors think me often alone, ~ and yet at such times I am in company with more than five hundred mutes ~ each of whom, at my pleasure, communicates his ideas to me by dumb signs ~ quite as intelligently as any person living can do by uttering of words.
~ *Laurence Sterne*

I like intellectual reading. It's to my mind what fiber is to my body.
~ *Grey Livingston*

You may have tangible wealth untold;
Caskets of jewels and coffers of gold.
Richer than I you can never be -
I had a mother who read to me.
~ *Strickland Gillilan (Thanks, Laurel)*

He who lends a book is an idiot. He who returns the book is more of an idiot.
~ *Arabic Proverb*

The mere brute pleasure of reading ~ the sort of pleasure a cow must have in grazing.
~ *Lord Chesterfield*

There is no such thing as a moral or immoral book; books are well written or badly written.
~ *Oscar Wilde, Picture of Dorian Gray, 1891*

An ordinary man can... surround himself with two thousand books... and thenceforward have at least one place in the world in which it is possible to be happy.
~ *Augustine Birrell*

We are too civil to books. For a few golden sentences we will turn over and actually read a volume of four or five hundred pages.
~ *Ralph Waldo Emerson*

From every book invisible threads reach out to other books; and as the mind comes to use and control those threads the whole panorama of the world's life, past and present, becomes constantly more varied and interesting, while at the same time the mind's own powers of reflection and judgment are exercised and strengthened.
~ *Helen E. Haines*

That is a good book which is opened with expectation and closed with profit.
~ *Amos Bronson Alcott*

Reading is to the mind what exercise is to the body. It is wholesome and bracing for the mind to have its faculties kept on the stretch.
~ *Augustus Hare*

A good book is the best of friends.
~ *English Proverb*

Books have to be read (worse luck it takes so long a time). It is the only way of discovering what they contain. A few savage tribes eat them, but reading is the only method of assimilation revealed to the West.
~ *E.M. Forster*

Except a living man there is nothing more wonderful than a book! A message to us from the dead, ~ from human souls whom we never saw, who lived perhaps thousands of miles away;

and yet these, on those little sheets of paper, speak to us, teach us, comfort us, open their hearts to us as brothers.
~ *Charles Kingsley*

Let your bookcases and your shelves be your gardens and your pleasure-grounds. Pluck the fruit that grows therein, gather the roses, the spices, and the myrrh.
~ *Judah Ibn Tibbon*

Books are a refuge, a sort of cloistral refuge, from the vulgarities of the actual world.
~ *Walter Pater*

A truly good book teaches me better than to read it. I must soon lay it down, and commence living on its hint.... What I began by reading, I must finish by acting.
~ *Henry David Thoreau*

A man may as well expect to grow stronger by always eating as wiser by always reading.
~ *Jeremy Collier*

> That place that does contain
> My books, the best companions, is to me
> A glorious court, where hourly I converse
> With the old sages and philosophers;
> And sometimes, for variety, I confer
> With kings and emperors, and weigh their counsels;
> Calling their victories, if unjustly got,
> Unto a strict account, and, in my fancy,
> Deface their ill-placed statues.
> ~ *Francis Beaumont and John Fletcher*

It often requires more courage to read some books than it does to fight a battle.
~ *Sutton Elbert Griggs*

> O for a Booke and a shdie nooke,
> eyther in-a-doore or out;
> With the grene leaves whisp'ring overhede,
> or the Streete cryes all about.
> Where I maie Reade all at my ease,
> both of the Newe and Olde;
> For a jollie goode Booke whereon to looke
> is better to me than Golde.
> ~ *John Wilson*

Books, not which afford us a cowering enjoyment, but in which each thought is of unusual daring; such as an idle man cannot read, and a timid one would not be entertained by, which even make us dangerous to existing institution ~ such call I good books.
~ *Henry David Thoreau*

Many persons read and like fiction. It does not tax the intelligence and the intelligence of most of us can so ill afford taxation that we rightly welcome any reading matter which avoids this.
~ *Rose Macaulay*

What holy cities are to nomadic tribes ~ a symbol of race and a bond of union ~ great books are to the wandering souls of men: they are the Meccas of the mind.
~ *G.E. Woodberry*

Reading ~ the best state yet to keep absolute loneliness at bay.
~ *William Styron*

A blessed companion is a book, ~ a book that, fitly chosen, is a lifelong friend, a book that, at a touch, pours its heart into our own.
~ *Douglas Jerrold*

A large, still book is a piece of quietness, succulent and nourishing in a noisy world, which I approach and imbibe with a sort of greedy enjoyment, as Marcel Proust said of those rooms of his old home whose air was saturated with the bouquet of silence.
~ *Holbrook Jackson*

'Tis the good reader that makes the good book; in every book he finds passages which seem confidences or asides hidden from all else and unmistakenly meant for his ear; the profit of books is according to the sensibility of the reader; the profoundest thought or passion sleeps as in a mine, until it is discovered by an equal mind and heart.
~ *Ralph Waldo Emerson, Society and Solitude, 1870*

We should read to give our souls a chance to luxuriate.
~ *Henry Miller*

The book of the moment often has immense vogue, while the book of the age, which comes in its company from the press, lies unnoticed; but the great book has its revenge. It lives to see its contemporary pushed up shelf by shelf until it finds its final resting-place in the garret or the auction room.
~ *Hamilton Wright Mabie*

The time to read is any time: no apparatus, no appointment of time and place, is necessary. It is the only art which can be practised at any hour of the day or night, whenever the time and

inclination comes, that is your time for reading; in joy or sorrow, health or illness.
~ *Holbrook Jackson*

All that mankind has done, though, gained or been: it is lying as in magic preservation in the pages of books.
~ *Thomas Carlyle*

I knew a gentleman who was so good a manager of his time that he would not even lose that small portion of it which the calls of nature obliged him to pass in the necessary-house; but gradually went through all the Latin poets in those moments.
~ *Lord Chesterfield*

This nice and subtle happiness of reading, this joy not chilled by age, this polite and unpunished vice, this selfish, serene life-long intoxication.
~ *Logan Pearsall Smith*

Books are delightful society. If you go into a room and find it full of books ~ even without taking them from the shelves they seem to speak to you, to bid you welcome.
~ *William Ewart Gladstone*

If minds are truly alive they will seek out books, for books are the human race recounting its memorable experiences, confronting its problems, searching for solutions, drawing the blueprints of it futures.
~ *Harry A. Overstreet*

The world of books is the most remarkable creation of man. Nothing else that he builds ever lasts. Monuments fall, nations perish, civilizations grow old and die out, and after an era new races build others. But in the world of books are volumes that have seen this happen again and again and yet live on, still young, still as fresh as the day they were written, still telling men's hearts of the heart of men centuries dead.

~ *Clarence Day*

I like books. I was born and bred among them, and have the easy feeling, when I get in their presence, that a stable-boy has among horses.

~ *Oliver Wendell Holmes*

I have lost all sense of home, having moved about so much. It means to me now ~ only that place where the books are kept.

~ *John Steinbeck*

The walls of books around him, dense with the past, formed a kind of insulation against the present world of disasters.

~ *Ross MacDonald*

Books are the ever burning lamps of accumulated wisdom.

~ *George William Curtis*

The books that help you most are those which make you think the most. The hardest way of learning is by easy reading: but a great book that comes from a great thinker~ it is a ship of thought, deep freighted with truth and with beauty.

~ *Theodore Parker*

# On Reading

To feel most beautifully alive means to be reading something beautiful, ready always to apprehend in the flow of language the sudden flash of poetry.
~ *Gaston Bachelard*

The reading of all good books is like conversation with the finest men of past centuries.
~ *Descartes*

Learning to read has been reduced to a process of mastering a series of narrow, specific, hierarchical skills. Where armed-forces recruits learn the components of a rifle or the intricacies of close order drill by the numbers, recruits to reading learn its mechanics sound by sound and word by word.
~ *Jacquelyn Gross*

Tell me what you read and I'll tell you who you are is true enough, but I'd know you better if you told me what you reread.
~ *François Mauriac*

Reading is a basic tool in the living of a good life.
~ *Mortimer J. Adler*

I am not a speed reader. I am a speed understander.
~ *Isaac Asimov*

The pleasure of reading is doubled when one lives with another who shares the same books.
~ *Katherine Mansfield*

Once we have learned to read, meaning of words can somehow register without consciousness.
~ *Anthony Marcel*

He had read much, if one considers his long life; but his contemplation was much more than his reading. He was wont to say that if he had read as much as other men he should have known no more than other men.
~ *John Aubrey*

If the riches of the Indies, or the crowns of all the kingdom of Europe, were laid at my feet in exchange for my love of reading, I would spurn them all.
~ *Francois FéNelon*

What is reading, but silent conversation.
~ *Walter Savage Landor*

Read, read, read. Read everything~ trash, classics, good and bad, and see how they do it. Just like a carpenter who works as an apprentice and studies the master. Read! You'll absorb it. Then write. If it is good, you'll find out. If it's not, throw it out the window.
~ *William Faulkner 1897-1962, American Novelist*

Happy is he who has laid up in his youth, and held fast in all fortune, a genuine and passionate love for reading.
~ *Rufus Choate 1799-1859, American Lawyer, Statesman*

The great objection to new books is that they prevent our reading old ones.
~ *Joseph Joubert*

In reading, as in eating, an appetite is half the feast.
~ *Anonymous*

Reading is not a duty, and has consequently no business to be made disagreeable.
~ *Augustine Birrell*

With one day's reading a man may have the key in his hands.
~ *Ezra Pound 1885-1972, American Poet, Critic*

Read good, big important things.
~ *Peggy Noonan 1950-, American Author, Presidential Speechwriter*

All that we have read and learned, all that has occupied and interested us in the thoughts and deeds of men abler or wiser than ourselves, constitutes at last a spiritual society of which we can never be deprived, for it rests in the heart and soul of the man who has acquired it.
~ *Philip Gilbert Hamilton*

Don't ask me who's influenced me. A lion is made up of the lambs he's digested, and I've been reading all my life.
~ *Giorgos Seferis*

How can you dare teach a man to read until you've taught him everything else first?
~ *George Bernard Shaw*

The power of a text is different when it is read from when it is copied out. Only the copied text thus commands the soul of him who is occupied with it, whereas the mere reader never discovers the new aspects of his inner self that are opened by the text, that road cut through the interior jungle forever closing behind it: because the reader follows the movement of his mind in the free flight of day-dreaming, whereas the copier submits it to command.
~ *Walter Benjamin*

The worst readers are those who behave like plundering troops: they take away a few things they can use, dirty and confound the remainder, and revile the whole.
~ *Friedrich Nietzsche 1844-1900, German Philosopher*

If I had read as much as other men I would have known no more than they.
~ *Thomas Hobbes*

Today a reader, tomorrow a leader.
~ *W. Fusselman*

Reading to kids is to ordinary reading what jazz is to a string quartet.
~ *Sean Wilentz, Reader's Quotation Book from Cool Quotes About Libraries Books and Knowledge*

To read is to fly: it is to soar to a point of vantage which gives a view over wide terrains of history, human variety, ideas, shared experience and the fruits of many inquiries.
~ *A C Grayling, Financial Times (in a review of A History of Reading by Alberto Manguel)*

Reading aloud with children is known to be the single most important activity for building the knowledge and skills they will eventually require for learning to read.
~ *Marilyn Jager Adams*

A capacity and taste for reading gives access to whatever has already been discovered by others.
~ *Abraham Lincoln*

The things I want to know are in books; my best friend is the man who'll get me a book I ain't read."
~ *Abraham Lincoln*

Research shows us that children who are read to from a very early age are more likely to begin reading themselves at an early age. They're more likely to excell in school. They're more likely to graduate secondary school and go to college.
~ *Laura Bush, UNESCO Speech, 2/28/05*

To read a writer is for me not merely to get an idea of what he says, but to go off with him and travel in his company.
~ *Andre Gide*

Reading a book is like re-writing it for yourself. You bring to a novel, anything you read, all your experience of the world. You bring your history and you read it in your own terms."
~ *Angela Carter*

Malnutrition of the reading faculty is a serious thing.
~ *Christopher Morley in The Haunted Bookshop*

To acquire the habit of reading is to construct for yourself a refuge from almost all of the miseries of life.
~ *W. Somerset Maugham*

Give me a man or woman who has read a thousand books and you give me an interesting companion. Give me a man or woman who has read perhaps three and you give me a dangerous enemy indeed.
~ *Anne Rice, The Witching Hour*

If you can read this, thank a teacher.
~ *Anonymous teacher*

Education... has produced a vast population able to read but unable to distinguish what is worth reading, an easy prey to sensations and cheap appeals.
~ *G. M. Trevelyan*

The habit of reading is the only enjoyment in which there is no alloy; it lasts when all other pleasures fade.
~ *Anthony Trollope*

All the best stories in the world are but one story in reality -- the story of escape. It is the only thing which interests us all and at all times, how to escape.
~ *Arthur Christopher Benson*

Wear the old coat and buy the new book."
~ *Austin Phelps*

The ability to read awoke inside me some long dormant craving to be mentally alive.
~ *Malcolm X, 1964, Autobiography*

The fluent reader sounds good, is easy to listen to, and reads with enough expression to help the listener understand and enjoy the material.
~ *Charles Clark, "Building Fluency: Do It Right and Do It Well!"* *(1999)*

You're the same today as you'll be in five years except for the people you meet and the books you read."
~ *Charlie "Tremendous" Jones*

I am not a speed reader.
I am a speed understander.
~ *Isaac Asimov*

There is creative reading as well as creative writing.
~ *Ralph Waldo Emerson*

When you sell a man a book you don't sell him just 12 ounces of paper and ink and glue ~ you sell him a whole new life.
~ *Christopher Morley*

It is better to read a little and ponder a lot than to read a lot and ponder a little.
~ *Denis Parsons Burkitt*

The reading of all good books is like conversation with the finest men of the past centuries.
~ *Descartes*

The connection between reading speed and comprehension; a film is made up of still images flashed in rapid succession to simulate movement. Slow down the film, and the movement and meaning slows and the film's impact is diminished. Viewers won't learn as much about the film as if it were shown at normal speed. With reading the same thing can happen.
When a person reads word by word, like frame by frame, they are not reading on the level of ideas. You need to read on some level that's more conversational and allows things to coalesce into ideas themselves.
~ *Doug Evans, Institute of Reading Development*

The more you read, the more things you will know. The more that you learn, the more places you'll go.
~ *Dr. Seuss, "I Can Read With My Eyes Shut!"*

Reading without reflecting is like eating without digesting.
~ *Edmund Burke*

This will never be a civilized country until we expend more money for books than we do for chewing gum.
~ *Elbert Hubbard*

The greatest gift is a passion for reading.
~ *Elizabeth Hardwick*

Children are made readers on the laps of their parents.
~ *Emilie Buchwald*

How my life has been brought to undiscovered lands, and how much richer it gets ~ all from words printed on a page.... How a book can have 560 pages, but in only three pages change the reader's life.

~ *Emoke B'Racz, Writing in Malaprop's Newsletter*

Once you learn to read, you will be forever free.

~ *Frederick Douglass*

Reading has given me more satisfaction than really anything else.

~ *Fashion designer Bill Blass, quoted in Worth (September 1999)*

Some people will lie, cheat, steal and back-stab to get ahead... and to think, all they have to do is READ.

~ *Fortune*

Only a generation of readers will span a generation of writers.

~ *Steven Spielberg*

The non-reading children are the greatest problem in American education.

~ *Glenn Doman, "How to Teach Your Baby to Read"*

Not all readers are leaders, but all leaders are readers.

~ *Harry S. Truman*

Teaching reading IS rocket science.

~ *Louisa Moats*

Reading takes us away from home, but more important, it finds homes for us everywhere.

~ *Hazel Rochman*

All evidence points to the seemingly illogical conclusion that the faster most people read, the better they understand."
~ *Harry Shefter, Faster Reading Self-Taught*

When I read about the evils of drinking, I gave up reading.
~ *Henny Youngman*

The goal in fluency instruction is not fast reading, although that happens to be a by-product of the instruction, but fluent meaning-filled reading.
~ *International Reading Association*

It is not enough to simply teach children to read; we have to give them something worth reading. Something that will stretch their imaginations--something that will help them make sense of their own lives and encourage them to reach out toward people whose lives are quite different from their own."
~ *Katherine Patterson*

Everyone probably thinks that I'm a raving nymphomaniac, that I have an insatiable sexual appetite, when the truth is I'd rather read a book.
~ *Madonna (1991)*

No entertainment is so cheap as reading, nor any pleasure so lasting. She will not want new fashions nor regret the loss of expensive diversions or variety of company if she can be amused with an author in her closet."
~ *Lady Mary Wortley Montagu 1689-1762, British Society Figure*

Reading is a discount ticket to everywhere.
~ *Mary Schmich*

A book is the most effective weapon against intolerance and ignorance.
~ *Lyndon Baines Johnson*

No one can read with profit that which he cannot learn to read with pleasure.
~ *Noah Porter*

Listening to good models of fluent reading, students can learn how a reader's voice can help text make sense.
~ *M.R. Kuhn & S.A. Stahl, "Fluency: A Review of Development and Remedial Practices" (2003)*

It has been established beyond a shadow of doubt that readers in general waste a great deal of time and effort.
~ *Manya and Eric De Leeuw, Read Better, Read Faster: A New Approach to Efficient Reading*

Every reader finds himself. The writer's work is merely a kind of optical instrument that makes it possible for the reader to discern what, without this book, he would perhaps never have seen in himself.
~ *Marcel Proust*

A text is at a students' independent reading level if they can read it with about 95% accuracy."
~ *Marie B. Clay, "An observation survey of early literacy achievement" (1993)*

As the child approaches a new text he is entitled to an introduction so that when he reads, the gist of the... story can provide some guide for a fluent reading.
~ *Marie B. Clay*

A good book is the best of friends, the same today and forever.
~ *Martin Tupper*

Reading gives us someplace to go when we have to stay where we are.
~ *Mason Cooley*

It is not true we have only one life to love, if we can read, we can live as many lives and as many kinds of lives as we wish.
~ *S.I. Hayakawa*

The man who reads nothing at all is better educated than the man who reads nothing but newspapers."
~ *Thomas Jefferson*

Let us read and let us dance ~ two amusements that will never do any harm to the world."
~ *Voltaire*

The first law of skillful reading is merely an application of the Law of Relative Importance. You must perceive, first of all, the total offerings of the printed matter; then you must appraise these.
~ *Walter Pitkin, The Art of Rapid Reading*

Reading makes a full man, meditation a profound man, discourse a clear man.
~ *Benjamin Franklin 1706-1790, American Scientist, Publisher*

What is reading but silent conversation?
~ *Walter Savage Landor*

The only thing better than good English writing is ~ I can't think of anything. You just don't pour it pureed over your potatoes. You savor it as if it were a fine chardonnay. What on Earth does it matter if you stop and repeat a phrase, roll it around on your tongue, dart a few lines ahead and then suddenly come back and reread it? If the phrase is good enough, you are supposed to stop and rejoice in it."
~ *William Murchison*

I'm sure we would not have had men on the Moon if it had not been for Wells and Verne and the people who write about this and made people think about it. I'm rather proud of the fact that I know several astronauts who became astronauts through reading my books.
~ *Arthur C. Clarke (1917 - ), Address to US Congress, 1975*

If you would not be forgotten, as soon as you are rotten, either write things worth reading or do things worth the writing.
~ *Benjamin Franklin (1706 - 1790)*

He has only half learned the art of reading who has not added to it the more refined art of skipping and skimming.
~ *Arthur James Balfour*

# On Authors

Of all the diversions of life, there is none so proper to fill up its empty spaces as the reading of useful and entertaining authors.
~ *Joseph Addison*

In comparing various authors with one another, I have discovered that some of the gravest and latest writers have transcribed, word for word, from former works, without making acknowledgment.
~ *Pliny the Elder (23 AD - 79 AD), Natural History*

The reading of all good books is indeed like a conversation with the noblest men of past centuries who were the authors of them, nay a carefully studied conversation, in which they reveal to us none but the best of their thoughts.
~ *Rene Descartes (1596 - 1650)*

It is a good thing for an uneducated man to read books of quotations. Bartlett's Familiar Quotations is an admirable work, and I studied it intently. The quotations when engraved upon the memory give you good thoughts. They also make you anxious to read the authors and look for more.
~ *Sir Winston Churchill (1874 - 1965), Roving Commission: My Early Life, 1930*

The genius of the United States is not best or most in its executives or legislatures, nor in its ambassadors or authors or colleges, or churches, or parlors, nor even in its newspapers or inventors, but always most in the common people.
~ *Walt Whitman (1819 - 1892)*

Quotations (such as have point and lack triteness) from the great old authors are an act of reverence on the part of the quoter, and a blessing to a public grown superficial and external.
~ *Louise Guiney*

This does not make the authors of those narratives liars; it makes them servants of fallible human memory and perception.
~ *Tom Bissell, Truth in Oxiana, 2004*

Nature, when she invented, manufactured and patented her authors, contrived to make critics out of the chips that were left.
~ *Oliver Wendell Holmes*

There are three difficulties in authorship: to write anything worth the publishing, to find honest men to publish it, and to get sensible men to read it.
~ *C. C. Colton*

Readers are less and less seen as mere non-writers, the subhuman other or flawed derivative of the author; the lack of a pen is no longer a shameful mark of secondary status but a positively enabling space …
~ *Terry Eagleton (1943 - ) British literary critic*

The idea that it is necessary to go to a university in order to become a successful writer … is one of those phantasies that surround authorship.
~ *Vera Brittain (1896 - 1970) English writer, poet, pacifist*

Though by whim, envy, or resentment led,
They damn those authors whom they never read.
~ *Charles Churchill (1731 - 1764) English poet, political journalist, clergyman*

Few books are more thrilling than certain confessions, but they must be honest, and the author must have something to confess.
~ *Simone de Beauvoir (1908 - 1986) French writer, The Second Sex, 1949.*

In England only uneducated people show off their knowledge; nobody quotes Latin or Greek authors in the course of conversation, unless he has never read them.
~ *George Mikes (1912 - 1987) British writer, How to be an Alien.*

What a sense of security in an old book which Time has criticized for us!
~ *James Russell Lowell (1819 - 1891) US poet, critic, editor, diplomat, My Study Windows, Library of Old Authors (1871).*

He who purposes to be an author, should first be a student.
~ *John Dryden (1631 - 1700) English poet, dramatist, critic*

I have turned my entire attention to Greek. The first thing I shall do, as soon as the money arrives, is to buy some Greek authors; after that, I shall buy clothes.
~ *Desiderius Erasmus (1469? - 1536) Dutch scholar, philosopher, author*

In quoting of books, quote such authors as are usually read; others you may read for your own satisfaction, but not name them.
~ *John Selden (1584 - 1654) English jurist, scholar, Table Talk, Books, Authors, 1686.*

To write it, it took three months; to conceive it -- three minutes; to collect the data in it -- all my life.
~ *F. Scott Fitzgerald (1896 - 1940) US author, The Author's Apology, Apr 1920, referring to his novel This Side of Paradise.*

The Muse of our Fiction of the future will lead you ~ if you are humble and honest with her ~ straight into a World of Working Men, crude of speech, swift of action, strong of passion, straight to the heart of a new life.
~ *Frank Norris (1870 - 1902) US novelist*

When I was a ten-year-old book worm and used to kiss the dust jacket pictures of authors as if they were icons, it used to amaze me that these remote people could provoke me to love.
~ *Erica Jong (1942 - ) US author, poet*

Age appears best in four things: old wood to burn, old wine to drink, old friends to trust, and old authors to read.
~ *Sir Francis Bacon*

My own experience is that once a story has been written, one has to cross out the beginning and the end. It is there that we authors do most of our lying ... one must ruthlessly suppress everything that is not concerned with the subject. If, in the first chapter, you say there is a gun hanging on the wall, you should make quite sure that it is going to be used further on in the story.
~ *Anton Chekhov*

Time is the author of authors.
~ *Sir Francis Bacon*

I was sorry to have my name mentioned as one of the great authors, because they have a sad habit of dying off. Chaucer is dead, Spenser is dead, so is Milton, so is Shakespeare, and I'm not feeling so well myself.
~ *Mark Twain*

Old wood best to burn, old wine to drink, old friends to trust, and old authors to read.
~ *Sir Sir Francis Bacon*

When Shakespeare is charged with debts to his authors, Landor replies, Yet he was more original than his originals. He breathed upon dead bodies and brought them into life.
~ *Ralph Waldo Emerson*

Author: A fool, who, not content with having bored those who have lived with him, insists on tormenting the generations to come.
~ *Montesquieu*

I should have no objection to a repetition of the same life from its beginning, only asking the advantages authors have in a second edition to correct some faults of the first.
~ *Benjamin Franklin (1706-1790)*

He who proposes to be an author should first be a student.
~ *John Dryden*

When you steal from one author, it's plagiarism; if you steal from many, it's research.
~ *Wilson Mizner (1876-1933)*

An author departs, he does not die.
~ *Dinah Maria Mulock*

Six characters in search of an author.
~ *Luigi Pirandello*

It is not until you are published that you realise that you really are what you wanted to be, an author!
~ *Anna Green*

We have not read an author till we have seen his object, whatever it may be, as he saw it.
~ *Thomas Carlyle*

I shall never be ashamed of citing a bad author if the line is good.
~ *Seneca*

I think of an author as somebody who goes into the marketplace and puts down his rug and says, 'I will tell you a story,' and then he passes the hat.
~ *Robertson Davies*

Poets are sultans, if they had their will: For every author would his brother kill.
~ *Roger Boyle*

The only happy author in this world is he who is below the care of reputation.
~ *Washington Irving*

What an author likes to write most is his signature on the back of a cheque.
~ *Brendan Francis Behan*

Born in a cellar... and living in a garret (The Author 1757)
~ *Samuel Foote*

Certainly the most diverse, if minor, pastime of literary life is the game of Find the Author.
~ *Arthur Miller*

No author ever drew a character consistent to human nature, but he was forced to ascribe to it many inconsistencies.
~ *Edward G. Bulwer-Lytton*

The author himself is the best judge of his own performance; none has so deeply meditated on the subject; none is so sincerely interested in the event.
~ *Edward Gibbon*

Cartesian: relating to Descartes, a famous philosopher, author of the celebrated dictum 'Cogito Ergo Sum'.
~ *Ambrose Bierce*

For two decades, the name of the author, Duncan Hines, was etched on the biting edge of the American appetite. The best-known and most purposeful vagabond.
~ *David Schwartz*

Critics are sentinels in the grand army of letters, stationed at the corners of newspapers and reviews, to challenge every new author.
~ *Henry Wadsworth Longfellow*

Every author really wants to have letters printed in the papers. Unable to make the grade, he drops down a rung of the ladder and writes novels.
~ *P G Wodehouse*

Choose an author as you choose a friend (Essay on Translated Verse)
~ *Earl Of Roscommon*

The great work must inevitably be obscure, except to the very few, to those who like the author himself are initiated into the mysteries. Communication then is secondary: it is perpetuation which is important. For this only one good reader is necessary.
~ *Henry Miller*

Making a book is a craft, like making a clock; it needs more than native wit to be an author.
~ *Jean De La Bruyere*

There is not less wit nor less invention in applying rightly a thought one finds in a book, than in being the first author of that thought.
~ *Pierre Bayle*

The virtue of dress rehearsals is that they are a free show for a select group of artists and friends of the author, and where for one unique evening the audience is almost expurgated of idiots.
~ *Alfred Jarry*

An author is a fool who, not content with boring those he lives with, insists on boring future generations.
~ *Charles Montesquieu*

In America the majority raises formidable barriers around the liberty of opinion; within these barriers an author may write what he pleases, but woe to him if he goes beyond them.
~ *Tocqueville*

And, after all, it is style alone by which posterity will judge of a great work, for an author can have nothing truly his own but his style.
~ *Isaac Disraeli*

The two most engaging powers of an author are to make new things familiar, familiar things new.
~ *William Makepeace Thackeray*

A critic is never too severe when he only detects the faults of an author. But he is worse than too severe when, in consequence of this detection, be presumes to place himself on a level with genius.
~ *Walter Landor*

Reading is an escape, an education, a delving into the brain of another human being on such an intimate level that every nuance of thought, every snapping of synapse, every slippery desire of the author is laid open before you like, well, a book.
~ *Cynthia Heimel*

Literary critics, however, frequently suffer from a curious belief that every author longs to extend the boundaries of literary art, wants to explore new dimensions of the human spirit, and if he doesn't, he should be ashamed of himself.
~ *Robertson Davies*

If you steal from one author, it's plagiarism. If you steal from two, it's research.
~ *John Burke*

What I like in a good author is not what he says but what he whispers.
~ *Logan Pearsall Smith*

Author A fool who, not content with having bored those who have lived with him, insists on tormenting generations to come.
~ *Montesquieu*

Have you ever observed that we pay much more attention to a wise passage when it is quoted than when we read it in the original author.
~ *Philip G. Hamerton*

If destruction be our lot we must ourselves be its author and finisher. As a nation of free men we must live through all time, or die by suicide.
~ *Abraham Lincoln*

Fixing our eyes on Jesus, the author and perfecter of faith, who for the joy set before Him endured the cross, despising the shame, and has sat down at the right hand of the throne of God.
~ *Hebrews 122 Bible*

In America the majority raises formidable barriers around the liberty of opinion within these barriers an author may write what he pleases, but woe to him if he goes beyond them.
~ *Aleksandr Isayevich Solzhenitsyn*

Real art is without irony. Irony distances the author from his material. Irony is a product of something. It's not the reason for doing something. Irony is a cheap shot.
~ *Robert Altman*

The author of the Iliad is either Homer or, if not Homer, somebody else of the same name.
~ *Aldous Huxley*

Whenever you read a good book, it's like the author is right there, in the room, talking to you, which is why I don't like to read good books.
~ *Jack Handey Deep Thoughts*

A good novel tells you the truth about its hero but a bad novel tells you the truth about its author.
~ *Gilbert Keith Chesterton*

A good novel tells us the truth about its hero but a bad novel tells us the truth about its author.
~ *G. K. Chesterton*

The one man who should never attempt an explanation of a poem is its author. If the poem can be improved by it's author's explanations it never should have been published, and if the poem cannot be improved by its author's explanations the explanations are scarcely worth reading.
~ *Archibald MacLeish*

Experience is an author's most valuable asset; experience is the thing that puts the muscle and the breath and the warm blood into the book he writes.
~ *Mark Twain, from Is Shakespeare Dead?, 1909*

An author ought to write for the youth of his generation, the critics of the next, and the schoolmasters of the afterward.
~ *Francis Scott Key Fitzgerald, aka F. Scott Fitzgerald*

Sleep on your writing; take a walk over it; scrutinize it of a morning; review it of an afternoon; digest it after a meal; let it sleep in your drawer a twelvemonth; never venture a whisper about it to your friend, if he be an author especially.
~ *Amos Bronson Alcott*

No moral system can rest solely on authority.
~ *A. J. Ayer, Humanist Outlook*

Reviewers are forever telling authors they can't understand them. The author might often reply: Is that my fault?
~ *A.W. Hare and J.C. Hare*

With him most authors steal their works, or buy; Garth did not write his own Dispensary.
~ *Alexander Pope*

History is a novel for which the people is the author.
~ *Alfred de Vigny, Réflexions sur la Vérité dans l'Art*

It is a safe rule to apply that, when a mathematical or philosophical author writes with a misty profundity, he is talking nonsense.
~ *Alfred North Whitehead*

My mother would say it is literally ghost writers who come to me.
~ *Amy Tan (author of what became The Joy Luck Club).*

Some authors should be paid by the quantity NOT written.
~ *Anonymous*

Those of us we have been true readers all our life fully realize the enormous extension of our being which we owe to authors"
~ *C.S. Lewis quotes (British Scholar and Novelist. 1898-1963)*

It is advantageous to an author that his book should be attacked as well as praised. Fame is a shuttlecock. If it be struck only at one end of the room, it will soon fall to the ground. To keep it up, it must be struck at both ends."
~ *Samuel Johnson (English Poet, Critic and Writer. 1709-1784)*

Age appears to be best in four things, ~ old wood best to burn, old wine to drink, old friends to trust, and old authors to read"
~ *Alonso of Aragon*

A creation of importance can only be produced when its author isolates himself, it is a child of solitude.
~ *Johann Wolfgang von Goethe (German Playwright, Poet, Novelist and Dramatist. 1749-1832)*

Without a humble imitation of the characteristics of the Divine Author of our blessed religion, we can never hope to be a happy nation.
~ *George Washington 1st US President (1789-97), 1732-1799)*

An author is a fool who, not content with having bored those who have lived with him, insists on boring future generation.
~ *Charles de Montesquieu (French Politician and Philosopher, 1689-1755)*

He who is the author of a war lets loose the whole contagion of hell and opens a vein that bleeds a nation to death.
~ *Thomas Paine (English born American Writer and political pamphleteer, whose 'Common Sense' and 'Crisis' papers were important influences on the American Revolution. 1737-1809)*

The authors of the gospels were unlettered and ignorant men and the teachings of Jesus have come to us mutilated, misstated and unintelligible"
~ *Thomas Jefferson quotes (American 3rd US President (1801-09).*

If a book comes from the heart it will contrive to reach other hearts. All art and author craft are of small account to that."
~ *Thomas Carlyle quotes (Scottish Historian and Essayist, leading figure in the Victorian era. 1795-1881)*

Writing is a difficult trade which must be learned slowly by reading great authors; by trying at the outset to imitate them; by daring then to be original; by destroying one's first productions.
~ *Andre Maurois (French Biographer, Novelist and Essayist, 1885-1967)*

Sit down and put down everything that comes into your head and then you're a writer. But an author is one who can judge his own stuff's worth, without pity, and destroy most of it.
~ *Sidonie Gabrielle*

Authors and actors and artists and such ~ Never know nothing, and never know much"
~ *Dorothy Parker (American short-story Writer and Poet, 1893-1967)*

Often while reading a book one feels that the author would have preferred to paint rather than write; one can sense the pleasure he derives from describing a landscape or a person, as if he were painting what he is saying, because deep in his heart he would have preferred to use brushes and colors."
~ *Pablo Picasso (Spanish Artist and Painter. 1881-1973)*

The most original authors are not so because they advance what is new, but because they put what they have to say as if it had never been said before.
~ *Johann Wolfgang von Goethe quotes (German Playwright, Poet, Novelist and Dramatist. 1749-1832)*

All mankind is of one author, and is one volume; when one man dies, one chapter is not torn out of the book, but translated into a better language; and every chapter must be so translated...As therefore the bell that rings to a sermon, calls not upon the preacher only, but upon the congregation to come: so this bell calls us all: but how much more me, who am brought so near the door by this sickness....No man is an island, entire of itself...any

man's death diminishes me, because I am involved in mankind; and therefore never send to know for whom the bell tolls; it tolls for thee."
~ *John Donne (English poet, 1572-1631)*

Adam was the author of sin, and I wish he had taken out an international copyright on it.
~ *Mark Twain (American Humorist and Writer.1835-1910)*

Authors like cats because they are such quiet, lovable, wise creatures, and cats like authors for the same reasons"
~ *Robertson Davies (Canadian Journalist and Author. 1913-1995)*

Theology made no provision for evolution. The biblical authors had missed the most important revelation of all! Could it be that they were not really privy to the thoughts of God?"
~ *Edward O. Wilson*

Every author in some way portrays himself in his works, even if it be against his will.
~ *Johann Wolfgang von Goethe (German Playwright, Poet, Novelist and Dramatist. 1749-1832)*

As an inspiration to the author, I do not think the cat can be over-estimated. He suggests so much grace, power, beauty, motion, mysticism. I do not wonder that many writers love cats; I am only surprised that all do not.
~ *Carl Van Vechten*

What makes a book great, a so-called classic, it its quality of always being modern, of its author, though he be long dead, continuing to speak to each new generation.
~ *Lawrence Clark Powell (American Librarian, Writer and Critic, 1906-2001)*

Every reader, if he has a strong mind, reads himself into the book, and amalgamates his thoughts with those of the author.
~ *Johann Wolfgang von Goethe quotes (German Playwright, Poet, Novelist and Dramatist. 1749-1832)*

To write what is worth publishing, to find honest people to publish it, and get sensible people to read it, are the three great difficulties in being an author.
~ *Charles Caleb Colton (English sportsman and writer, 1780-1832)*

# On Libraries

I have always imagined that Paradise will be a kind of library.
~ *Jorge Luis Borges (1899-1986) Argentine poet, short-story writer*

> . . . if those only wrote, who were
> sure of being read, we should have
> fewer authors;
> and the shelves of libraries
> would not groan beneath the weight
> of dusty tomes more voluminous
> than luminous.
> ~ *Lady Marguerite Blessington (1789-1849),*
> *English socialite, writer The Confessions of an*
> *Elderly Lady, 1838.*

A newspaper is a circulating library with high blood pressure.
~ *Bugs Baer (1886-1969) U.S. journalist*

The library is the temple of learning, and learning has liberated more people than all the wars in history.
~ *Carl Thomas Rowan*

If past history was all there was to the game, the richest people would be librarians.
~ *Warren Buffett 1930 - U.S. business executive*

A library is thought in cold storage.
~ *Herbert Samuel*

I am what libraries and librarians have made me, with little assistance from a professor of Greek and poets.
~ *B. K. Sandwell*

I learned 3 important things in college to use a library, to memorize quickly and visually, to drop asleep any time given a horizontal surface and 15 minutes. What I could not learn was to think creatively on schedule.
~ *Agnes George DeMille 1905-U.S. dancer, choreographer*

Life is a library owned by an author. It has a few books which he wrote himself, but most of them were written for him.
~ *Harry Emerson Fosdick (1878 - 1969) US clergyman*

The library is like a place of sacredness. If we were fools at onetime, perhaps we will not be fools tomorrow, if we study.
~ *Chief Tom Porter*

Librarians are not just good at internet searching because we understand how to play word games. We're good because we know where we need to go and the quickest routes for getting there; we are equipped not just with compasses but with mental maps of the information landscape.
~ *Marylaine Block*

We are drowning in information but starved for knowledge.
~ *John Naisbitt*

Research is the process of going up alleys to see if they are blind.
~ *Marston Bates*

I heard his library burned down and both books were destroyed...and one of them hadn't even been colored in yet.
~ *John Dawkins*

Doing research on the Web is like using a library assembled piecemeal by pack rats and vandalized nightly.
~ *Roger Ebert*

Libraries are reservoirs of strength,
grace and wit, reminders of order,
calm and continuity,
lakes of mental energy,
neither warm nor cold,
light nor dark.
The pleasure they give is steady,
unorgastic, reliable,
deep and long-lasting.
~ *Germaine Greer 1939-*

T'is true: there's magic in the web of it...
~ *William Shakespeare, Othello Act 3, Scene 4*

My Alma mater was books, a good library I could spend the rest
of my life reading, just satisfying my curiosity.
~ *Malcolm X (1925-1965) U.S. political activist*

The great British Library ~ one of these sequestered pools of
obsolete literature to which modern authors repair, and draw
buckets full of classic lore, or pure English, undefiled wherewith
to swell their own scanty rills of thought.
~ *Washington Irving (1783-1859) U.S. short-story writer, essayist, The
Sketch-Book, The Art of Book-Making, 1819-20.*

A library, to modify the famous metaphor of Socrates, should be
the delivery room for the birth of ideas—a place where history
comes to life.
~ *Norman Cousins*

> I acknowledge immense debt to the griots
> [tribal poets] of Africa --
> where today it is rightly said
> that when a griot dies,
> it is as if a library has burned
> to the ground.
> ~ *Alex Haley (1921-1992) U.S. novelist, journalist*

If I were founding a university I would begin with a smoking
room; next a dormitory; and then a decent reading room and a
library. After that, if I still had more money that I couldn't use, I
would hire a professor and get some text books.
~ *Stephen Leacock (1869-1944) Canadian author*

Yes, there's such a thing as luck in trial law but it only comes at 3 o'clock in the morning You'll still find me in the library looking for luck at 3 o'clock in the morning.
~ *Louis Nizer (1902-1994) English lawyer*

He who learns, and makes no use of his learning, is a beast of burden with a load of books. Does the ass comprehend whether he carries on his back a library or a bundle of faggots?
~ *Moslih Eddin Saadi (1184-1291) Persian poet*

When I step into this library, I cannot understand why I ever step out of it.
~ *Marie de Sevigne (1626-1696) French diarist*

To a historian libraries are food, shelter, and even muse.
~ *Barbara W. Tuchman (1912-1989) U.S. historian*

As the biggest library if it is in disorder is not as useful as a small but well-arranged one, so you may accumulate a vast amount of knowledge but it will be of far less value than a much smaller amount if you have not thought it over for yourself.
~ *Arthur Schopenhauer (1788-1860) German philosopher*

Even in life [Sinclair Lewis] was fully alive only in his writing. He lives in public libraries from Maine to California, in worn copies in the bookshelves of women from small towns who, in their girlhood, imagined themselves as Carol Kennicotts.
~ *Dorothy Thompson (1894-1961) U.S. journalist, writer, The Boy from Sauk Center, Atlantic, Nov 1960.*

If truth is beauty, how come no one has their hair done in a library?
~ *Lily Tomlin (1939- ) U.S. actress, comedienne*

Just the omission of Jane Austen's books alone would make a fairly good library out of a library that hadn't a book in it.
~ *Mark Twain (1835 - 1910)*

The closest thing we will ever come to an orderly universe is a good library.
~ *Ashleigh Brilliant*

Don't be afraid to go in your library and read every book.
~ *Dwight D. Eisenhower*

Access to knowledge is the superb, the supreme act of truly great civilizations. Of all the institutions that purport to do this, free libraries stand virtually alone in accomplishing this mission.
~ *Toni Morrison*

Anyone who has a library and a garden wants for nothing.
~ *Marcus Tullius Cicero*

Throughout my formal education I spent many, many hours in public and school libraries. Libraries became the courts of last resort, as it were. The current definitive answer to almost any question can be found within the four walls of most libraries.
~ *Arthur Ashe*

Everything you need for better future and success has already been written. And guess what? All you have to do is go to the library.
~ *Jim Rohn*

I think the health of our civilization, the depth of our awareness about the underpinnings of our culture and our concern for the future can all be tested by how well we support our libraries.
~ *Carl Sagan*

A library should be like a pair of open arms.
~ *Roger Rosenblatt*

A library is the delivery room for the birth of ideas, a place where history comes to life.
~ *Norman Cousins, Bettman, Otto L. The Delights of Reading: Quotes, Notes, & Anecdotes. David R. Godine, Publisher, Inc. Boston: 1987.*

The libraries of America are and must ever remain the home of the free, inquiring minds. To them, our citizens ~ of all ages and races, of all creeds and political persuasions ~ must ever be able to turn with clear confidences that there they can freely seek the whole truth, unwarped by fashion and uncompromised by expediency.
~ *Dwight D. Eisenhower, Letter to the American Library Association's Annual Conference. Los Angeles: 1953.*

More people should use their library.
~ *Regis Philbin*

If this nation is to be wise as well as strong, if we are to achieve our destiny, then we need more new ideas for more wise men reading more good books in more public libraries. These libraries should be open to all—except the censor. We must know all the facts and hear all the alternatives and listen to all the criticisms. Let us welcome controversial books and controversial authors. For the Bill of Rights is the guardian of our security as well as our liberty.
~ *John Fitzgerald Kennedy (American 35th US President (1961-63), 1917-1963)*

What can I say? Librarians rule.
~ *Regis Philbin*

A library implies an act of faith.
~ *Victor Hugo*

A library is a hospital for the mind.
~ *Anonymous*

We English majors...need to promote public libraries as a tool in the war against terror. How many readers of Edith Wharton have engaged in terroristic acts? I challenge you to name one...Do we need to wait until our cities lie in smoking ruins before we wake up to the fact that a first-class public library is a vital link in national defense?
~ *Garrison Keillor*

A library is but the soul's burying ground. It is a land of shadows.
~ *Henry Ward Beecher*

The quantity of books in a person's library, is often a cloud of witnesses to the ignorance of the owner.
~ *Count Axel Gustafsson Oxenstierna*

There are seventy million books in American libraries, but the one you want is always out.
~ *Thomas L. Masson*

A library is not a luxury but one of the necessities of life.
~ *Henry Ward Beecher*

More than a building that houses books and data, the library represents a window to a larger world, the place where we've always come to discover big ideas and profound concepts that help move the American story forward and the human story forward.
~ *Barack Obama, Keynote address at the American Library Association's Annual Conference. Chicago. 2005*

The way an old dog finds his way back over miles and miles to his home when somebody trues to shove him off on a farm someplace, that is how I find my way back to the library. It's my place, even more than my place is.
~ *Chris Lynch, Whitechurch. HarperTeen: New York, 2000*

There are times when I think that the ideal library is composed solely of reference books. They are like understanding friends-always ready to change the subject when you have had enough of this or that.
~ *James Donald Adams*

A good library is a palace where the lofty spirits of all nations and generations meet.
~ *Samuel Niger*

The public library is the most dangerous place in town.
~ *John Ciardi*

The libraries have become my candy store.
~ *Juliana Kimball*

If information is the currency of democracy, then libraries are the banks.
~ *Wendell Ford*

Instead of going to Paris to attend lectures, go to the public library, and you won't come out for twenty years, if you really wish to learn.
~ *Leo Tolstoy*

A circulating library in a town is an evergreen tree of diabolical knowledge!
~ *Richard Brinsley Sheridan*

To a historian libraries are food, shelter, and even muse. They are of two kinds: the library of published material, books, pamphlets, periodicals, and the archive of unpublished papers and documents.
~ *Barbara W. Tuchman*

We should burn all libraries and allow to remain only that which everyone knows by heart. A beautiful age of the legend would then begin.
~ *Hugo Ball*

I did it! And it's all thanks to the books at my local library.
*(Futurama, The Day the Earth Stood Stupid episode, 2001. Line spoken by the character of Fry.)*

An hour spent in the library is worth a month in the laboratory.
~ *Anonymous*

My library was dukedom large enough.
~ *William Shakespeare (The Tempest)*

What do we, as a nation, care about books? How much do you think we spend altogether on our libraries, public or private, as compared with what we spend on our horses?
~ *John Ruskin*

What is more important in a library than anything else ~ than everything else ~ is the fact that it exists.
~ *Archibald Macleish*

Your library is your paradise.
~ *Desiderius Erasmus*

A man should keep his little brain attic stocked with all the furniture that he is likely to use, and the rest he can put away in the lumber room of his library, where he can get it if he wants it.
~ *Sir Arthur Conan Doyle*

A man's library is a sort of harem.
~ *Ralph Waldo Emerson*

Be a little careful about your library. Do you foresee what you will do with it? Very little to be sure. But the real question is, What it will do with you? You will come here and get books that will open your eyes, and your ears, and your curiosity, and turn you inside out or outside in.
~ *Ralph Waldo Emerson*

Here Greek and Roman find themselves alive along these crowded shelves; and Shakespeare treads again his stage, and Chaucer paints anew his age.
~ *John Greenleaf Whittier*

I go into my library, and all history unrolls before me. I breathe the morning air of the world while the scent of Eden's roses yet lingered in it, while it vibrated only to the world's first brood of nightingales, and to the laugh of Eve. I see the pyramids building; I hear the shoutings of the armies of Alexander.
~ *Alexander Smith*

A library is an arsenal of liberty.
~ *Unknown*

I've been drunk for about a week now, and I thought it might sober me up to sit in a library.
~ *Anonymous*

It is almost everywhere the case that soon after it is begotten the greater part of human wisdom is laid to rest in repositories.
~ *Georg C. Lichtenberg*

Show me a computer expert that gives a damn, and I'll show you a librarian.
~ *Patricia Wilson Berger (Chicago Tribune article, 29 June 1990)*

Libraries are reservoirs of strength, grace and wit, reminders of order, calm and continuity, lakes of mental energy, neither warm nor cold, light nor dark. The pleasure they give is steady, unorgastic, reliable, deep and long-lasting. In any library in the world, I am at home, unselfconscious, still and absorbed.
~ *Germaine Greer*

The medicine chest of the soul.
~ *Library at Thebes, inscription over the door*

Madam, a circulating library in a town is as an evergreen tree of diabolical knowledge; it blossoms through the year. And depend on it that they who are so fond of handling the leaves, will long for the fruit at last.
~ *Richard Brinsley Sheridan*

Meek young men grow up in libraries, believing it their duty to accept the views which Cicero, which Locke, which Bacon, have given, forgetful that Cicero, Locke, and Bacon were only young men in libraries, when they wrote these books. Hence, instead of Man Thinking, we have the book-worm.
~ *Ralph Waldo Emerson*

No place affords a more striking conviction of the vanity of human hopes than a public library.
~ *Samuel Johnson*

Some on commission, some for the love of learning, some because they have nothing better to do or because they hope these walls of books will deaden the drumming of the demon in their ears.
~ *Louis Macneice*

The great British Library ~ an immense collection of volumes of all ages and languages, many of which are now forgotten, and most of which are seldom read: one of these sequestered pools of obsolete literature to which modern authors repair, and draw buckets full of classic lore, or "pure English, undefiled" wherewith to swell their own scanty rills of thought.
~ *Washington Irving*

To add a library to a house is to give that house a soul.
~ *Cicero*

I received the fundamentals of my education in school, but that was not enough. My real education, the superstructure, the details, the true architecture, I got out of the public library. For an impoverished child whose family could not afford to buy books, the library was the open door to wonder and achievement, and I can never be sufficiently grateful that I had the wit to charge through that door and make the most of it.
~ *Isaac Asimov*

Libraries are as the shrine where all the relics of the ancient saints, full of true virtue, and that without delusion or imposture, are preserved and reposed.
~ *Sir Francis Bacon*

If it is noticed that much of my outside work concerns itself with libraries, there is an extremely good reason for this. I think that the better part of my education, almost as important as that secured in the schools and the universities, came from libraries.
~ *Irving Stone*

There is a growing view, however, that the strands of community life are unravelling ~ violence, alcohol and drug use, crime, alienation, degradation of the political process, and ineffectual social institutions are increasingly accepted as inevitable. Computers and communication technology are often touted as saviours of the modern age, but the benefits of the 'computer revolution' are unevenly distributed and the lack of access to communication technology contributes to the widening gulf between socioeconomic classes.
~ *D. Schulder, Community Networks, 1994*

Librarians are almost always very helpful and often almost absurdly knowledgeable. Their skills are probably very underestimated and largely underemployed.
~ *Charles Medawar*

I do miss [politics] sometimes, I actually miss sitting in Roehampton library on a Saturday afternoon trying to help people sort out their problems.
~ *David Mellor, 1997*

The true university these days is a collection of books.
~ *Thomas Carlyle*

Make thy books thy companions. Let thy cases and shelves be thy pleasure grounds and gardens.
~ *Judah ibn-Tibbon (12th century)*
Give thy mind to books and libraries, and the literature and lore of the ages will give thee the wisdom of sage and seer.
~ *Newell D. Hillis*

I go into my library and all history unrolls before me.
~ *Alexander Smith*

A library of wisdom, then, is more precious than all wealth, and all things that are desirable cannot be compared to it.
~ *Richard de Bury*

It is, however, not to the museum, or the lecture-room, or the drawing-school, but to the library, that we must go for the completion of our humanity. It is books that bear from age to age the intellectual wealth of the world.
~ *Owen Meredith, from Inspirational Quotes About Libraries, Librarians and Book Collections*

Perhaps no place in any community is so totally democratic as the town library. The only entrance requirement is interest.
~ *Lady Bird Johnson*

The only true equalisers in the world are books; the only treasure-house open to all comers is a library; the only wealth which will not decay is knowledge; the only jewel which you can carry beyond the grave is wisdom.
~ *J. A. Langford*

The library, I believe, is the last of our public institutions to which you can go without credentials... You don't even need the sticker on your windshield that you need to get into the public beach. All you need is the willingness to read.
~ *Harry Golden*

And even should the cloud of barbarism and despotism again obscure the science and libraries of Europe, this country remains to preserve and restore light and liberty to them.
~ *Thomas Jefferson*

Nothing sickens me more than the closed door of a library.
~ *Barbara W. Tuchman*

Your library is your portrait.
~ *Holbrook Jackson*

They are the books, the arts, the academes, That show, contain and nourish all the world.
~ *William Shakespeare, Love's Labour's Lost*

A circulating library in a town is as an evergreen tree of diabolical knowledge! It blossoms through the year!
~ *Richard Brainsley Sheridan*

Knowing I lov'd my books, he furnish'd me,
~ *Shakespeare, The Tempest*

I myself spent hours in the Columbia library as intimidated and embarrassed as a famished gourmet invited to a dream restaurant where every dish from all of the world's cuisines, past and present, was available on request.
~ *Luigi Barzini*

Second hand books are wild books, homeless books; they have come together in vast flocks of variegated feather, and have a charm which the domesticated volumes of the library lack.
~ *Virginia Woolf*

But what can a man see of a library being one day in it?
~ *James Boswell*

The dissemination of knowledge is one of the cornerstones of civilization.
~ *John F. Budd*

The man who has a library of his own collection is able to contemplate himself objectively, and is justified in believing in his own existence.
~ *Augustine Birrell*

Come, and take choice of all my library,
And so beguile thy sorrow.
~ *William Shakespeare, Titus Andronicus*

What is a great love of books? It is something like a personal introduction to the great and good men of all past times. Books, it is true, are silent as you see them on their shelves; but, silent as they are, when I enter a library I feel as if almost the dead were present, and I know if I put questions to these books they will answer me with all the faithfulness and fullness which has been left in them by the great men who have left the books with us.
~ *John Bright*

Life is like a library owned by an author. In it are a few books which he wrote himself, but most of them were written for him.
~ *Harry Emerson Fosdick*

It is impossible to enter a large library... without feeling an inward sensation of reverence, and without catching some sparks of noble emulation, from the mass of mind which is scattered around you.
~ *James Crossley*

The reflections and histories of men and women throughout the world are contained in books.... America's greatness is not only recorded in books, but it is also dependent upon each and every citizen being able to utilize public libraries.
~ *Terence Cooke (1921-1983)*

As regards anything besides these, my son, take a warning: To the making of many books there is no end, and much devotion to them is wearisome to the flesh.
~ *Eccleslastese 12:12 (New World Translation 1961)*

For whatever is truly wondrous and fearful in man, never yet was put into words or books.
~ *Herman Melville, Moby Dick, chapter 110*

My lifelong love affair with books and reading continues unaffected by automation, computers, and all other forms of the twentieth-century gadgetry.
~ *Robert Downs (1903- ) Books in My Life*

Two forces are successfully influencing the education of a cultivated man: art and science. Both are united in the book.
~ *Maksim Gorky (1868-1936)*

A library book...is not, then, an article of mere consumption but fairly of capital, and often in the case of professional men, setting out in life, is their only capital.
~ *Thomas Jefferson (1743-1826)*

A house without books is like a room without windows. No man has a right to bring up children without surrounding them with books.... Children learn to read being in the presence of books.
~ *Horace Mann (1796-1859)*

When you come, bring the cloak that I left with Carpus at Troas, also the books, and above all the parchments.
~ *2 Timothy 4:13, St. Paul to his son Timothy*

'Tis well to borrow from the good and great;
'Tis wise to learn; 'tis God-like to create!
~ *John Godfrey SAXE (1816-1887), The Library*

A good library is a place, a palace where the lofty spirits of all nations and generations meet.
~ *Samuel Niger (1883-1956)*

He was inspired, and yet he wants books!
He had been preaching for thirty years, and yet he wants books!
He had seen the Lord, and yet he wants books!
He had a wider experience than most men do, and yet he wants books!
He had been caught up into the third heaven, and had heard things that it was not lawful for a man to utter, and yet he wants books!
He had written a major part of the New Testament, and yet he wants books!
~ *C.H. Spurgeon in an 1863 sermon,*
*Paul - His Cloak and His Books*

A great public library, in its catalogue and its physical disposition of its books on shelves, is the monument of literary genres.
~ *Robert Melcanon (1947- ) Cited in World Literature Today, 1982*

Children, don't speak so coarsely,' said Mr Webster, who had a vague notion that some supervision should be exercised over his daughters' speech, and that a line should be drawn, but never knew quite when to draw it. He had allowed his daughters to use his library without restraint, and nothing is more fatal to maidenly delicacy of speech than the run of a good library.
~ *Robertson Davies Tempest Tost*

For him that stealeth a Book from this Library, let it change into a serpent in his hand and rend him. Let him be struck with Palsy, and all his Members blasted. Let him languish in Pain crying aloud for Mercy and let there be no sur-cease to his Agony till he sink in Dissolution. Let Bookworms gnaw his Entrails in token of the Worm that dieth not, and when at last he goeth to his final Punishment, let the flames of Hell consume him for ever and aye.
~ *Curse Against Book Stealers, Monastery of San Pedro, Barcelona*
*(Actually a hoax from the Old Librarians Almanack)*

My experience with public libraries is that the first volume of the book I inquire for is out, unless I happen to want the second, when that is out.
~ *Oliver Wendell Holmes (1809-1894), The Poet at the Breakfast Table*

My father gave me free run of his library. When I think of my boyhood, I think in terms of the books I read.
~ *Jorge Luis Borges (1899-1986)*

Classification, broadly defined, is the act of organizing the universe of knowledge into some systematic order. It has been considered the most fundamental activity of the human mind.
~ *Lois Mai Chan, Cataloguing and Classification: An Introduction*

Consider what you have in the smallest chosen library. A company of the wisest and wittiest men that could be picked out of all civil countries, in a 1000 years, have set in best order the results of their learning and wisdom. The men themselves were hid and inaccessible, solitary, impatient of interruption, fenced by etiquette; but the thought which they did not uncover to their bosom friend is here written out in transparent words to us, the strangers of another age.
~ *Ralph Waldo Emerson (1803-1882) Books. Society and Solitude*

Shera's Two Laws of Cataloguing.
Law #1 No cataloger will accept the work of any other cataloger.
Law #2 No cataloger will accept his/her own work six months after the cataloging.
~ *Jesse Shera University of Illinois, Graduate School of Library Science.*

A university is just a group of buildings gathered around a library.
~ *Shelby Foote*

It does not matter how many books you may have, but whether they are good or not.
~ *Lucius Annaeus Seneca (3 B.C.-65 A.D.), Epistolae Morale*

It is clear that censorship is not a cut and dried issue. There is a danger in thinking it is, for then the debate falters and understanding ends. We must realize that censorship will be with us always. It is a weapon to protect the order of society and the peace of communities. However, it is a two-edged sword and must be handled with care and caution. Of all professions librarianship must ensure that both sides of the debate remain alive. If the censorship side predominates, truth and moral progress suffer; if the anti-censorship side predominates, the drift to selfishness and anarchy presents a clear danger to the cohesion and order of the social system, the destruction of which brings us to barbarism, tyranny, and the loss of all freedom.
~ *S.D. Neill, A Clash of Values: Censorship, Canadian Library Journal*

When a librarian really believes that a book is harmful, that its content is contrary to the welfare of the community, or that it is destructive of good taste, even if those are his opinions only, he has not only the right, but also the obligation to do what he properly can to keep that book out of the hand of those whom he thinks might be injured by it.
~ *Jesse Shera, Intellectual Freedom~ Intellectual? Free? Wilson Library Bulletin, Nov. 1967, 323-4, 345.*

Throughout my formal education I spent many, many hours in public and school libraries. Libraries became courts of last resort, as it were. The current definitive answer to almost any question can be found within the four walls of most libraries.
~ *Arthur Ashe (1943-1993)*

No possession can surpass, or even equal a good library, to the lover of books. Here are treasured up for his daily use and delectation, riches which increase by being consumed, and pleasures that never cloy.
~ *John Alfred Landoford (1823-1903)*

The library connects us with the insight and knowledge, painfully extracted from Nature, of the greatest minds that ever were, with the best teachers, drawn from the entire planet and from all our history, to instruct us without tiring, and to inspire us to make our own contribution to the collective knowledge of the human species. I think the health of our civilization, the depth of our awareness about the underpinnings of our culture and our concern for the future can all be tested by how well we support our libraries.
~ *Carl Sagan, Cosmos*

In my day the library was a wonderful place.... We didn't have visual aids and didn't have various programs...it was a sanctuary.... So I tend to think the library should remain a center of knowledge.
~ *Norman Mailer (1923- ) Cited in American Libraries, July/August 1980, p.411-412*

Children's books are written for upbringing...but upbringing is a great thing; it decides the fate of the human being.
~ *Vissarion Grigor'evich Belinskii (1811-1841)*

Every library should try to be complete on something, if it were only the history of pinheads.
~ *Oliver Wendell Holmes (1809-1894), The Poet at the Breakfast Table. VIII.*

The first thing naturally when one enters a scholar's study or library, is to look at his books. One gets the notion very speedily of his tastes and the range of his pursuits by a glance round his book-shelves.
~ *Oliver Wendell Holmes (1809-1894), The Poet at the Breakfast Table. VIII.*

Knowing that I loved my books, he furnished me,
~ *William Shakespeare (1564-1616), The Tempest.*

The library is not a shrine for the worship of books. It is not a temple where literary incense must be burned or where one's devotion to the bound book is expressed in ritual. A library, to modify the famous metaphor of Socrates, should be the delivery room for the birth of ideas ~ a place where history comes to life.
~ *Norman Cousins (1915- ), Cited in ALA Bulletin, Oct. 1954, p.475*

A factor and trader for helps to learning.
~ *John Dury*

A man will turn over half a library to make one book.
~ *Samuel Johnson (1709-1784, Life of Johnson. From James Boswell, April 6, 1775.*

Libraries are the wardrobes of literature, whence men, properly informed may bring forth something for ornament, much for curiosity, and more for use.
~ *William Dyer (1636-1696)*

Man, the imperfect librarian, may be the product of chance or of malevolent demiurgi; the universe, with its elegant endowment of shelves, of enigmatical volumes, of inexhaustible stairways for the traveller and latrines for the seated librarian, can only be the work of a god.
~ *Jean Luis Borges (1899-1986), The Library of Babel, Labyrinths*

The librarian of today, and it will be true still more of the librarians of tomorrow, are not fiery dragons interposed between the people and the books. They are useful public servants, who manage libraries in the interest of the public... Many still think that a great reader, or a writer of books, will make an excellent librarian. This is pure fallacy.
~ *Sir William Osler, 1917*

Librarian is a service occupation. Gas station attendant of the mind.
~ *Richard Powers, In The Gold Bug Variations p.35, 1991.*

As eunuchs are the guardians of the fair.
~ *Edward Young (1684-1765), Love of Fame. Satire ii. L. 83.*

A library represents the mind of its collector, his fancies and foibles, his strength and weakness, his prejudices and preferences. Particularly is this the case if to the character of a collector he adds ~ or tries to add- the qualities of a student who wishes to know the books and the lives of the men who wrote them. The friendships of his life, the phases of his growth, the vagaries of his mind, all are represented.
~ *Sir William Osler, 1919*

Nutrimentum spiritus. (Food for the soul.)
~ *Inscription on the Berlin Royal Library.*

Libraries are as the shrines where all the relics of the ancient saints, full of true virtue, and that without delusion or imposture, are preserved and reposed.
~ *Sir Francis Bacon (1561-1626)*

I declare after all there is no enjoyment like reading! How much sooner one tires of anything than of a book! When I have a house of my own, I shall be miserable if I have not an excellent library.
~ *Jane Austen (1775 - 1817), Pride and Prejudice, 1811*

A little library growing each year is an honorable part of a man's history.
~ *Henry Ward Beecher*

A library is but the soul's burial-ground. It is the land of shadows.
~ *Henry Ward Beecher, Star Papers. Oxford. Bodleian Library.*

A great library contains the diary of the human race.
~ *George Mercer Dawson (1849-1901), Address on Opening the Birmingham Free Library*

New Laws of Librarianship:
Libraries serve humanity.
Respect all forms by which knowledge is communicated.
Use technology intelligently to enhance service.
Protect free access to knowledge.
Honor the past & create the future.
~ *Michael Gorman (American Libraries 9/95)*

My books are very few, but then the world is before me ~ a library open to all ~ from which poverty of purse cannot exclude me ~ in which the meanest and most paltry volume is sure to furnish something to amuse, if not to instruct and improve.
~ *Joseph Howe, Letter to George Johnson, January 1824.*

Si, ténte par le demon,
Tu dérobes ce livre,
Souviens-toi qu'un fripon
N'est pas digne de vivre.
~ *Anonymous*

A library is like an island in the middle of a vast sea of ignorance, particularly if the library is very tall and the surrounding area has been flooded.
~ *David Handler*

A democratic society depends upon an informed and educated citizenry.
~ *Thomas Jefferson (1743-1826)*

Ranganathan's Five Laws:
Books are for use.
Books are for all; or Every reader his book.
Every book its reader.
Save the time of the reader.
A library is a growing organism.
~ *Shiyali Ramamrita Ranganathan (1892-1972)*

Th' first thing to have in a libry is a shelf. Fr'm time to time this can be decorated with lithrachure. But th' shelf is th' main thing.
~ *Finley Peter Dunne (1867-1936), Books. Mr Dooley Says.*

You see, I don't believe that libraries should be drab places where people sit in silence, and that's been the main reason for our policy of employing wild animals as librarians.
~ *Monty Python skit*

I have always imagined that Paradise will be a kind of library.
~ *Jorge Luis Borges (1899-1986)*

What a place to be in is an old library! It seems as though all the souls of all the writers that have bequeathed their labours to these Bodleians were reposing here as in some dormitory, or middle state. I do not want to handle, to profane the leaves, their winding-sheets. I could as soon dislodge a shade. I seem to inhale

learning, walking amid their foliage; and the odor of their old moth-scented coverings is fragrant as the first bloom of the sciential apples which grew amid the happy orchard.
~ *Charles Lamb (1775-1834), Essays of Elia.*

The librarian's mission should be, not like up to now, a mere handling of the book as an object, but rather a know how (mise au point) of the book as a vital function.
~ *Jose Ortegay Gasset (1883-1955) Mission del Bibliotecario*

Shelved around us lie
The mummied authors.
~ *Baynard Taylor (1825-1878), Third Evening. The Poet's Journal.*

Thou can'st not die. Here thou art more than safe
Where every book is thy epitaph.
~ *Henry Vaughan (1621-1695), On Sir Thomas Bodley's library*

Here, then, is the point at which I see the new mission of the librarian rise up incomparably higher than all those preceding. Up until the present, the librarian has been principally occupied with the book as a thing, as a material object. From now on he must give his attention to the book as a living function. He must become a policeman, master of the raging book.
~ *Jose Ortegay Gasset (1883-1955), A translation of OyG's address to the International Congress of Bibliographers and Librarians in Paris in 1934.*

Mary Kay is one of the secret masters of the world: a librarian. They control information. Don't ever piss one off.
~ *Spider Robinson, The Callahan Touch*

Believers and doers are what we need ~ faithful librarians who are humble in the presence of books.... To be in a library is one of the purest of all experiences. This awareness of library's unique, even sacred nature, is what should be instilled in our neophytes.
~ *Lawrence Clark Powell (1906- ), A Passion for Books*

I am what the librarians have made me with a little assistance from a professor of Greek and a few poets.
~ *Bernard Keble Sandwell (1876-1954), Learning and Society*

One frequently finds,
Lower their voices
And raise their minds.
~ *Richard Armour*

You must live feverishly in a library. Colleges are not going to do any good unless you are raised and live in a library everyday of your life.
~ *Ray Douglas Bradbury (1920- ), Cited in Writer's Digest, February 1976*

There was one place where I forgot the cold, indeed forgot Siberia. That was in the library. There, in that muddy village, was a great institution. Not physically, to be sure, but in every other way imaginable. It was a small log cabin, immaculately attended to with loving care; it was well lighted with oil lamps and it was warm. But best of all, it contained a small but amazing collection from the world's best literature, truly amazing considering the time, the place, and its size. From floor to ceiling it was lined with books ~ books, books, books. It was there that I was to become

acquainted with the works of Dumas, Pasternak's translations of Shakespeare, the novels of Mark Twain, Jack London, and of course the Russians. It was in that log cabin that I escaped from Siberia ~ either reading there or taking the books home. It was between that library and two extraordinary teachers that I developed a lifelong passion for the great Russian novelists and poets. It was there that I learned to line up patiently for my turn to sit at a table and read, to wait ~ sometimes months ~ for a book. It was there that I learned that reading was not only a great delight, but a privilege.
~ *Esther Hautzig*

There is not such a cradle of democracy upon the earth as the Free Public Library, this republic of letters, where neither rank, office, nor wealth receives the slightest consideration.
~ *Andrew Carnegie*

The student has his Rome, his Florence, his whole glowing Italy, within the four walls of his library. He has in his books the ruins of an antique world and the glories of a modern one.
~ *Henry Wadsworth Longfellow (1807-1882)*

What a school thinks about its library is a measure of what it thinks about education.
~ *Harold Howe, former U.S. Commissioner of Education*

Students who score higher on tests tend to come from schools which have more library resource staff and more books, periodicals and videos, and where the instructional role of the teacher-librarian and involvement in cooperative program planning and teaching is more prominent.
~ *Keith Curry Lance, et. al. The Impact of School Library Media Centers on Academic Achievement.*

The reflections and histories of men and women throughout the world are contained in books....America's greatness is not only recorded in books, but it is also dependent upon each and every citizen being able to utilize public libraries.
~ *Terence Cooke (1921-1983)*

I've been drunk for about a week now, and I though it might sober me up to sit in a library.
~ *F. Scott Fitzgerald (1896-1948), The Great Gatsby, chapter 3*

The public library has been historically a vital instrument of democracy and opportunity in the United States.... Our history has been greatly shaped by people who read their way to opportunity and achievements in public libraries.
~ *Arthur Meier Schlesinger (1888-1965)*

So the America I loved still exists, if not in the White House or the Supreme Court or the Senate or the House of Representatives or the media. The America I love still exists at the front desks of our public libraries.
~ *Kurt Vonnegut, In These Times, 2004*

The richest minds need not large libraries.
~ *Amos Bronson Alcott, Table Talk. Bk. I. Learning - Book*

It is vanity to persuade the world one hath much learning, by getting a great library.
~ *Thomas Fuller (1608-1661), The Holy and Profane States*

What is more important in a library than anything else ~ than everything else ~ is the fact that it exists.
~ *Archibald MacLeish, The Premise of Meaning, American Scholar*

The best of my education has come from the public library... my tuition fee is a bus fare and once in a while, five cents a day for an overdue book. You don't need to know very much to start with, if you know the way to the public library.
~ *Lesley Conger*

Perhaps no place in any community is so totally democratic as the town library. The only entrance requirement is interest.
~ *Lady Bird Johnson*

As a child, my number one best friend was the librarian in my grade school. I actually believed all those books belonged to her.
~ *Erma Bombeck*

We may sit in our library and yet be in all quarters of the earth. ~ *John Lubbock*

A library is but the soul's burial-ground. It is the land of shadows.
~ *Henry Ward Beecher*

To those with ears to hear, libraries are really very noisy places. On their shelves we hear the captured voices of the centuries-old conversation that makes up our civilization.
~ *Timothy Healy*

If you have a garden and a library, you have everything you need.
~ *Marcus Tullius Cicero*

I love the place; the magnificent books; I require books as I require air.
~ *Sholem Asch*

The richest person in the world ~ in fact all the riches in the world ~ couldn't provide you with anything like the endless, incredible loot available at your local library.
~ *Malcolm Forbes*

A good library will never be too neat, or too dusty, because somebody will always be in it, taking books off the shelves and staying up late reading them.
~ *Lemony Snicket*

The library is not a shrine for the worship of books. It is not a temple where literary incense must be burned or where one's devotion to the bound book is expressed in ritual. A library, to modify the famous metaphor of Socrates, should be the delivery room for the birth of ideas ~ a place where history comes to life.
~ *Norman Cousins*

A truly great library contains something in it to offend everyone.
~ *Jo Godwin*

Consider what you have in the smallest chosen library. A company of the wisest and wittiest men that could be picked out of all civil countries, in a thousand years, have set in best order the results of their learning and wisdom. The men themselves were hid and inaccessible, solitary, impatient of interruption, fenced by etiquette; but the thought which they did not uncover to their bosom friend is here written out in transparent words to us, the strangers of another age.
~ *Ralph Waldo Emerson, Books, Society and Solitude*

A university is just a group of buildings gathered around a library.
~ *Shelby Foote*

What a place to be in is an old library! It seems as though all the souls of all the writers that have bequeathed their labours to these Bodleians were reposing here as in some dormitory, or middle state. I do not want to handle, to profane the leaves, their winding-sheets. I could as soon dislodge a shade. I seem to inhale learning, walking amid their foliage; and the odor of their old moth-scented coverings is fragrant as the first bloom of the sciential apples which grew amid the happy orchard.
~ *Charles Lamb, Essays of Elia*

No possession can surpass, or even equal a good library, to the lover of books. Here are treasured up for his daily use and delectation, riches which increase by being consumed, and pleasures that never cloy.
~ *John Alfred Landford*

Libraries are reservoirs of strength, grace and wit, reminders of order, calm and continuity, lakes of mental energy, neither warm nor cold, light nor dark.... In any library in the world, I am at home, unselfconscious, still and absorbed.
~ *Germaine Greer*

Librarian is a service occupation. Gas station attendant of the mind.
~ *Richard Powers*

The student has his Rome, his Florence, his whole glowing Italy, within the four walls of his library. He has in his books the ruins of an antique world and the glories of a modern one.
~ *Henry Wadsworth Longfellow*

The library connects us with the insight and knowledge, painfully extracted from Nature, of the greatest minds that ever were, with the best teachers, drawn from the entire planet and from all our history, to instruct us without tiring, and to inspire us to make our own contribution to the collective knowledge of the human species. I think the health of our civilization, the depth of our awareness about the underpinnings of our culture and our concern for the future can all be tested by how well we support our libraries.
~ *Carl Sagan, Cosmos*

Libraries are not made; they grow.
~ *Augustine Birrell, London: 1887.*

Without libraries what have we? We have no past and no future.
~ *Ray Bradbury (American science-fiction short stories and novels writer, 1920)*

If truth is beauty, how come no one has their hair done in a library.
~ *Lily Tomlin (American Actress and Comedian. Mark Twain Prize for American Humor in 2003.b.1939)*

A public library is the most enduring of memorials, the trustiest monument for the preservation of an event or a name or an affection; for it, and it only, is respected by wars and revolutions, and survives them.
~ *Mark Twain (American Humorist, Writer and Lecturer. 1835-1910)*

I may not be an explorer, or an adventurer, or a treasure-seeker, or a gunfighter, Mr. O'Connell, but I am proud of what I am...I, am a librarian!!
~ *From the movie, The Mummy*

That perfect tranquillity of life, which is nowhere to be found but in retreat, a faithful friend and a good library.
~ *Aphra Behn (English dramatist, novelist, and poet, 1640-1689)*

To those with ears to hear, libraries are really very noisy places. On their shelves we hear the captured voices of the centuries-old conversation that makes up our civilization.
~ *Timothy Healy*

Libraries are not made, they grow.
~ *Augustine Birrell quotes*

Libraries are the one American institution you shouldn't rip off.
~ *Barbara Kingsolver quotes (American Writer and Activist. b.1955)*

No university in the world has ever risen to greatness without a correspondingly great library... When this is no longer true, then will our civilization have come to an end.
~ *Lawrence Clark Powell (American Librarian, Writer and Critic, 1906-2001)*

My books are very few, but then the world is before me ~ a library open to all ~ from which poverty of purse cannot exclude me ~ in which the meanest and most paltry volume is sure to furnish something to amuse, if not to instruct and improve.
~ *Joseph Howe*

A library, to modify the famous metaphor of Socrates, should be the delivery room for the birth of ideas ~ a place where history comes to life.
~ *Norman Cousins (American Essayist and Editor, long associated with the Saturday Review. 1912-1990)*

A great library contains the diary of the human race.
~ *George Mercer Dawson*

A man should keep his little brain attic stocked with all the furniture that he is likely to use, and the rest he can put away in the lumber-room of his library, where he can get it if he wants it.
~ *Arthur Conan Doyle, Sr. (Scottish writer, creator of the detective Sherlock Holmes, 1859-1930)*

I myself spent hours in the Columbia library as intimidated and embarrassed as a famished gourmet invited to a dream restaurant where every dish from all the world's cuisines, past and present, was available on request.
~ *Luigi Barzine*

No place affords a more striking conviction of the vanity of human hopes than a public library; for who can see the wall crowded on every side by mighty volumes, the works of laborious meditations and accurate inquiry, now scarcely known...
~ *Samuel Johnson quotes (English Poet, Critic and Writer. 1709-1784)*

A library is a delivery room for the birth of ideas, a place where history comes to life.
~ *Norman Cousins*

As a child, my number one best friend was the librarian in my grade school. I actually believed all those books belonged to her.
~ *Erma Bombeck*

A man's library is a sort of harem.
~ *Ralph Waldo Emerson, The Conduct of Life*

My books are very few, but then the world is before me a library open to all from which poverty of purse cannot exclude me in which the meanest and most paltry volume is sure to furnish something to amuse, if not to instruct and improve.
~ *Joseph Howe*

The library is not a shrine for the worship of books. It is not a temple where literary incense must be burned or where one's devotion to the bound book is expressed in ritual. A library, to modify the famous metaphor of Socrates, should be the delivery room for the birth of ideas~ a place where history comes to life.
~ *Norman Cousins*

There are 70 million books in American libraries, but the one I want to read is always out.
~ *Tom Masson (1866-1934)*

A Library that is not accessible out of business hours is of as little value as gold horded in a vault and withdrawn from circulation.
~ *Alexander Graham Bell (letter to Mabel Hubbard Bell, 17 Nov. 1896)*

A new library is like finding a $100 bill on the sidewalk.
~ *Anonymous library patron*

A perverse mind presides over the holy defense of the library.
~ *Umberto Eco (The Name of the Rose. HBJ, 1983, p. 176)*

Away with lamentation! Away with elegies and dirges! Away with biographies and histories, and libraries and museums! Let the dead be the dead.
~ *Henry Miller*

Blaming the library for exposure to pornography is like blaming the lake if your child walks up to it alone, falls in and then drowns.
~ *David Sawyer (Spokane Spokesman-Review, 18 Dec. 2000)*

Doing research on the Web is like using a library assembled piecemeal by pack rats and vandalized nightly.
~ *Roger Ebert (Yahoo! Internet Life column, Sept. 1998, p. 66)*

I always dreamed you'd be my library buddy.
~ *The Simpsons episode. (Line spoken by the character of Lisa Simpson)*

I accept the risk of damnation. The Lord will absolve me, because He knows I acted for His glory. My duty was to protect the library.
~ *Umberto Eco (The Name of the Rose. HBJ, 1983, p. 471)*

I assumed he could not resist the temptation to penetrate the library and look at the books.
~ *The Name of the Rose, 1986 (Dwight Weist as voice of old Adson.)*

I did most of my learning in the library, where I could go at my own pace. I learned that I really could be a scientist and that I could take risks that other students couldn't because nobody had any expectations of me.
~ *John Jack Horner, paleontologist (Chicago Tribune article, 23 January 2003)*

I don't like libraries and I don't like dealing with librarians. They say they want change, but what they want is what they had in the past.
~ *Frank Gehry, architect (Chicago Tribune article, 20 August 2004)*

I was born on a shelf in the rare books library.
~ *Janis Ian (Belle of the Blues)*

I'd like to be in charge of a library, or be an archeologist. Again, it's research, a bit of detective work ~ the things I really love to do.
~ *Bill Wyman (Publishers Weekly interview, 9 Sept. 2002, p. 53)*

If you want to get laid, go to college, but if you want an education, go to the library.
~ *Frank Zappa*

If you didn't want them to think, you shouldn't have given them library cards.
~ *Robert Kaufman (Getting Straight, dir. Richard Rush, 1970)*

It's one thing to be in a bookstore. But to see your book in a library, to me that really means something.
~ *David Sedaris (Public Libraries interview)*

We cannot have good libraries until we first have good librarians ~ properly educated, professionally recognized, and fairly rewarded.
~ *Herbert S. White (Library Journal column, 15 Nov. 1999)*

We must conceive of the library as a channel through which books pass on their way from the publisher to the incinerator.
~ *G. Hardin, 1947 (New York Times article, 26 October 2002)*

Where any nation starts awake Books are the memory. And it's plain Decay of libraries is like Alzheimer's in the nation's brain.
~ *Ted Hughes (Hear It Again)*

In the houses of the humble a little library in my opinion is a most precious possession.
~ John Bright

No possession can surpass, or even equal, a good library to the lover of books.
~ *J. A. Langford*

Me, poor man, my library
Was dukedom large enough.
~ *William Shakespeare, The Tempest*

A little library, growing larger every year, is an honourable part of a man's history. It is a man's duty to have books. A library is not a luxury, but one of the necessaries of life.
~ *Henry Ward Beecher*

The library of a good man is one of his most constant, cheerful, and instructive companions; and as it has delighted him in youth, so will it solace him in old age.
~ *C. Frognall Dibdin*

How still and peaceful is a Library! It seems quiet as the grave, tranquil as heaven, a cool collection of the thoughts of the men of all times. And yet, approach and open the pages, and you find them full of dissension and disputes, alive with abuse and detraction— a huge, many-volumed satire upon man, written by himself... What a broad thing is a library — all shades of opinion reflected on its catholic bosom, as the sunbeams and shadows of a summer's day upon the ample mirror of a lake.
~ *George Gilfillan*

Every man should have a library....And when we have got our little library we may look proudly at Shakspeare, and Bacon, and Bunyan, as they stand in our bookcase in company with other noble spirits, and one or two of whom the world knows nothing, but whose worth we have often tested. These may cheer and enlighten us, may inspire us with higher aims and aspirations, may make us, if we use them rightly, wiser and better men.
~ *William A. E. Axon*

Knowledge is of two kinds. We know a subject ourselves, or we know where we can find information upon it. When we enquire into any subject, the first thing we have to do, is to know what books have treated of it. This leads us to look at catalogues, and the backs of books in libraries.
~ *Samuel Johnson*

A scholar must shape his own shell, secrete it, one might almost say, for secretion is only separation, you know, of certain elements derived from the materials of the world about us. And a scholar's study, with the books lining its walls, is his shell.
~ *Oliver Wendell Holmes*

In my garden I spend my days; in my library I spend my nights. My interests are divided between my geraniums and my books. With the flower I am in the present; with the book I am in the past. I go into my library, and all history unrolls before me.
~ *Alexander Smith*

The truest owner of a Library is he who has bought each book for the love he bears to it; who is happy and content to say,— Here are my jewels; my choicest material possessions.
~ *Frank Carr*

A very short examination of a library is sufficient to enable one to describe the owner in general and unmistakable terms.
~ *Author Unkown*

My guess is (it will be) about 300 years until computers are as good as, say, your local reference library in search.
~ *Craig Silverstein, director of technology, Google.com*

One of the greatest gifts my brother and I received from my mother was her love of literature and language. With their boundless energy, libraries open the door to these worlds and so many others. I urge young and old alike to embrace all that libraries have to offer.

~ *Caroline Kennedy*

My encouragement to you is to go tomorrow to the library.

~ *Maya Angelou, Poet (during a speech to a college audience that encouraged students to read voraciously and never stop learning).*

Libraries are community treasure chests, loaded with a wealth of information available to everyone equally, and the key to that treasure chest is the library card. I have found the most valuable thing in my wallet is my library card.

~ *Laura Bush (former First Lady)*

Those who declared librarians obsolete when the Internet rage first appeared are now red-faced. We need them more than ever. The Internet is full of 'stuff' but its value and readability is often questionable. 'Stuff' doesn't give you a competitive edge, high-quality related information does.

~ *Patricia Schroeder, Association of American Publishers President*

I used to go to the library all the time when I was kid. As a teenager, I got a book on how to write jokes at the library, and that, in turn, launched my comedy career.

~ *Drew Carey (Comedian, Carey donated nearly $600,000 to the Ohio Library Council).*

In hard times, libraries are more important than ever. Human beings need what books give them better than any other medium. Since ancient nights around prehistoric campfires, we have needed myth. And heroes. And moral tales. And information about the world beyond the nearest mountains or oceans.

Today, with books and movies more expensive than ever, and television entertainment in free fall to the lowest level of stupidity, free circulating books are an absolute necessity. They are quite simply another kind of food. For those without money, the road to the treasure house of the imagination begins at the public library.
~ *Pete Hamill, Columnist New York Daily News*

My childhood library was small enough not to be intimidating. And yet I felt the whole world was contained in those two rooms. I could walk any aisle and smell wisdom.
~ *Rita Dove, U.S. Poet Laureate*

Being in the library is so addictive for me that I really have to exercise self-control so I can get some writing done at home.
~ *Janet Fitch, Author of White Oleander*

Libraries are places where we writers go after we die, if we're lucky. We?re going to live on through libraries. But there is also something more. In addition to being a place that we go after we die, if we are lucky, libraries are also the place where a great many writers are born. ~ *Joe Klein, author of Primary Colors and The Running Mate*

The library (in the migrant community) I grew up in was my only link to the outside world.
~ *Luis Valdez, Playwright and filmmaker*

When we build a public library, we don't have to pay to get in, but when we build a stadium, we have to pay the owner every time we go to a game.
~ *Jesse Ventura, Minnesota Governor*

It was a great place to write a novel about book burning, in the library basement.
~ *Ray Bradbury on writing his classic novel Fahrenheit 45, 50 years ago.*

I would walk into the Carnegie Library and I would see the pictures of Booker T. and pictures of Frederick Douglass and I would read. I would go into the Savannah Public Libraries in the stacks and see all of the newspapers from all over the country. Did I dream that I would be on the Supreme Court? No. But I dreamt that there was a world out there that was worth pursuing.
~ *Clarence Thomas, U.S. Supreme Court Justice*

The public library is more than a repository of books. It's a mysterious, wondrous place with the power to change lives.
~ *Elizabeth Taylor, Chicago Tribune literary editor*

Many librarians perform their duties with a profound sense of responsibility: supporting the foundations of democracy by ensuring free access to information.
~ *John Schwartz, New York Times reporter*

Libraries are my passion in life. Before I became mayor (of Los Angeles), I used to sneak out here during lunchtime...and I'd go to a corner and take a book~ any book almost~ and read it for a while, and then feel rejuvenated.
~ *Richard Riordan*

But despite the meek, shush-shushing stereotype, librarians are largely a freedom-upholding, risk-taking group. In the name of the First Amendment and anti-censorship, they have championed the causes of provocative writers and spoken out against banned and challenged books.
~ *Linton Weeks, writer Washington Post*

It's an essential fight librarians are making, an age-old fight; yours is a battle for civilization. It's a fight for our country's founding values.
~ *Jim Hightower, Radio talk-show host*

My very identities as a reader and a writer began at the Walt Whitman branch library.
~ *Paula Spencer, Woman's Day Contributing Editor*

Books and reading saved a very lonely childhood. At the library I found people who took interest in me. From books, I learned about people and compassion.
~ *Nancy Slonim Aronie, Author of Writing from the Heart*

You must live feverishly in a library. Colleges are not going to do any good unless you are raised and live in a library every day of your life.
~ *Ray Bradbury*

As a child I was a very shy little blonde kid that didn't speak at all to anybody...And what was wonderful about the library was that you didn't have to say a word. So it was my oasis. And you didn't have to ask for things in full sentences. You could just point to a shelf and say, '18th century dolls,' and the librarians would lead you there. It was amazing. I felt like a queen.
~ *Adrienne Yorinks, award-winning illustrator and quilter.*

I find that when I come out of the library I'm in what I call the library bliss of being totally taken away from the distractions of life.
~ *Tracy Chevalier, Author of Girl with a Pearl Earring*

I fell in love with libraries when I first walked into the school library in Falls City, Texas, population 462. It was tiny and I quickly read through almost everything, but it was a lifeline for a child starved for a larger world. In many ways I owe great chunks of the life I lead to libraries.
~ *Jane Chestnutt, Editor-in-Chief, Woman's Day Magazine*

I liked reading and working out my ideas in the midst of that endless crowd walking in and out of the (library) looking for something. I, too, was seeking fame and fortune by sitting at the end of a long golden table next to the sets of American authors on the open shelves.
~ *Alfred Kazin, author*

I have relied on the library to provide the research materials for five books and uncountable magazine articles. But what has always impressed me most forcefully is the institution's connection to the everyday life of New Yorkers, from giggling teenagers to the very old...From its beginnings, this (library) building has served both as an instigator and a mirror of social change. The Library is one of the last bastions of respect for those who try to carry on...independent scholarship...As a writer, I can never get over the sense of being absolutely lucky to be able to get my hands (literally) on so many books.
~ *Susan Jacoby, writer*

Going to the library builds a kid's imagination. Books help them discover themselves and the world.
~ *Mike Bordick, Baltimore Oriole All-Star shortstop*

Teenagers can discover the pleasures of reading and gain the power of knowledge by going to libraries. With that power, they will be invincible.
~ *Ward Burton, NASCAR driver, winner of the Daytona 500.*

We must not think of learning as only what happens in schools. It is an extended part of life. The most readily available resource for all of life is our public library system.
~ *David McCullough, Author*

What is more important in a library than anything else-than everything else-is the fact that it exists.
~ *Archibald MacLeish, Poet*

Getting my library card was like citizenship; it was like American citizenship.
~ *Oprah Winfrey*

When I was a kid and the other kids were home watching Leave it to Beaver, my father and step-mother were marching me off to the library.
~ *Oprah Winfrey*

The richest person in the world ~ in fact. All the riches in the world ~ couldn't provide you with anything like the endless, incredible loot available at your local library. You can measure the awareness, the breadth and the wisdom of a civilization, a nation, a people by the priority given to preserving these repositories of all that we are, all that we were, or will be.
~ *Malcolm Forbes, Publisher*

My alma mater was books, a good library.
~ *Malcolm X*

When you are growing up, there are two institutional places that affect you most powerfully-the church, which belongs to God, and the public library, which belongs to you. The public library is a great equalizer.

~ *Keith Richards, Musician*

The part of my education that has had the deepest influence wasn't any particular essay or even a specific class, it was how I was able to apply everything I learned in the library to certain situations in my life... The library takes me away from my everyday life and allows me to see other places and learn to understand other people unlike myself.

~ *Gloria Estefan, Musician*

As a child, I loved to read books. The library was a window to the world, a pathway to worlds and people far from my neighborhood in Philadelphia. And even today, as I travel around the world, I often visit places I used to dream about because of the books I'd read. The library made a difference in my life.

~ *Ed Bradley, Broadcaster*

The free access to information is not a privilege, but a necessity for any free society. One of my favorite things to do as a young man was wander through the stacks of my hometown library. I'd just browse until I found something interesting. Libraries have definitely changed my life.

~ *Edward Asner, Actor*

When I was young, we couldn't afford much. But, my library card was my key to the world.

~ *John Goodman, Actor*

Whatever the cost of our libraries, the price is cheap compared to that of an ignorant nation.
~ *Walter Cronkite, Broadcaster*

We all love to hear a good story. We save our stories in books. We save our books in libraries. Libraries are the storyhouses full of all those stories and secrets.
~ *Kathy Bates, Actor*

I am here because libraries and museums are singular and important institutions with unique contributions to make to our nation. But more importantly, I am here as an advocate for children and families, for healthy communities, for economic development, for scholars and researchers, for individuals who seek educational and informational resources throughout their lives.
~ *Robert Martin, Former U.S. Institute of Museum and Library Services Director*

The day I discovered that one could go to the public library and take out books was one of the happiest of my life.
~ *Liz Smith, Columnist*

The library is not only a diary of the human race, but marks an act of faith in the continuity of humanity.
~ *Vartan Gregorian, President, Carnegie Corporation*

There are ways to recover one's perspective. You can wait for one of those periodic crisis that summon the best of the decent men and women who toil at virtually every level of government. Or you can go to your local public library, where the democratic ideals of liberty, equality, and free inquiry are still burnished by daily use.
~ *Brian Dickerson, Columnist Detroit Free Press*

I think the New York Public Library is so, so amazing. It's literally the coolest place ~ It's good shelter from the sun and it's the most beautiful building. It's really, really fun.
~ *Natalie Portman, Actress*

Public libraries have been a mainstay of my life. They represent an individual's right to acquire knowledge; they are the sinews that bind civilized societies the world over. Without libraries, I would be a pauper, intellectually and spiritually.
~ *James A. Michener, Author*

When I was a child in the Navy during World War II, I was perennially grateful to the armed services libraries for having on hand a good supply of those pocket books, which were so common in that period. I must have read a couple hundred of them, and they did a lot to save my sanity.
~ *James A. Michener, Author*

If you tell even a single librarian joke, I'm outta here.
~ *Josephine Carr (The Dewey Decimal System of Love. New American Library, 2003, p. 37)*

Librarians have always been among the most thoughtful and helpful people. They are teachers without a classroom. No libraries, no progress.
~ *Willard Scott, Broadcaster*

Libraries store the energy that fuels the imagination. They open up windows to the world and inspire us to explore and achieve, and contribute to improving our quality of life. Libraries change lives for the better.
~ *Sidney Sheldon, Author*

The library is our house of intellect, our transcendental university, with one exception: no one graduates from a library. No one possibly can, and no one should.
~ *Vartan Gregorian, President, Carnegie Corporation*

We are not mere gatekeepers and doorkeepers of humanity's heritage. We also must protect its dissemination. We must beware of all censorship in whatever form it comes, because to censor, to tamper with truth, to tamper with our memory, is to commit a historical sin. We, as librarians, have a major duty that we must all share all over the world, in order not to allow anybody to control, to twist, and most important of all, to manipulate our human will and through it our free institutions.
~ *Vartan Gregorian, President, Carnegie Corporation*

Beware the lustful fires that burn in a librarian's heart. They can rage beyond all control.
~ *The Onion (Fire Safety and Prevention Tips, 28 May 2003)*

The library is central to our free society. It is a critical element in the free exchange of information at the heart of our democracy.
~ *Vartan Gregorian, President, Carnegie Corporation*

Access to knowledge is the superb, the supreme act of truly great civilizations. Of all the institutions that purport to do this, free libraries stand virtually alone in accomplishing this mission. No committee decides who may enter, no crisis of body or spirit must accompany the entrant. No tuition is charged, no oath sworn, no visa demanded. Of the monuments humans build for themselves, very few say touch me, use me, my hush is not indifference, my space is not barrier. If I inspire awe, it is because I am in awe of you and the possibilities that dwell in you.
~ *Toni Morrison, Author*

I'm of a fearsome mind to throw my arms around every living librarian who crosses my path, on behalf of the souls they never knew they saved.
~ *Barbara Kingsolver, Author*

Here was one place where I could find out who I was and what I was going to become. And that was the public library.
~ *Jerzy Kosinski, Author*

When I got my library card, that's when my life began.
~ *Rita Mae Brown, Author*

Censorship, like charity, should begin at home; but unlike charity, it should end there.
~ *Clare Booth Luce*

Libraries promote the sharing of knowledge, connecting people of all ages with valuable information resources. These dynamic and modern institutions, and the librarians who staff them, add immeasurably to our quality of life.
~ *President George W. Bush*

Burnout for librarians seems to me both foolish and unnecessary. Work hard, work well, work effectively. Work until quitting time. Then go home and enjoy the rest of your life. If that leaves an unsolved problem, tell your boss on the way out the door or write the boss a note.
~ *Herbert S. White (At the Crossroads. Libraries Unlimited, 1995, p. 210)*

<u>Library</u>
Here is where people
One frequently finds
And raise their mind
~ *Richard Armour*

And, guys have this thing with librarians: 'I really like frumpy librarians with glasses who, after a couple of tequila shots, take their hair out of the bun and get crazy.'
~ *Sonya Jury, architect (Quoted in Construction.com article, 5 December 2002)*

As a general rule, librarians are a kick in the pants socially, often full of good humor, progressive, and, naturally, well read.
~ *Bill Hall (As quoted in American Libraries, January 2002, p. 44)*

Our whole American way of life is a great war of ideas, and librarians are the arms dealers selling weapons to both sides.
~ *James Quinn (WESTPAC/NOCALL joint meeting, 1990)*

I deserve a swift kick in the shorts for all the times I've stubbornly wound my way through the library stacks, my mule head leading the way, searching fruitlessly for information a librarian could put in my hands in a matter of minutes.
~ *Michael Perry (Handbook for Freelance Writing, 1995, as quoted in Marylaine Block's Ex Libris, 23 February 2001)*

I just knew I wanted to be respected. I wanted to be good at sport. I wanted to be pretty. I wanted to be head librarian.
~ *Lucy Lawless (Quoted in Sydney Morning Herald article, 30 January 1999)*

In fact a few simple mathematical calculations reveal that if reference librarians were paid at market rates for all the roles they play, they would have salaries well over $200,000.
~ *Will Manley (The Truth About Reference Librarians. McFarland, 1996)*

In the nonstop tsunami of global information, librarians provide us with floaties and teach us how to swim.
~ *Linton Weeks (Washington Post article, 13 January 2001, p. C01)*

Langdon had been inside hermetic vaults many times, but it was always an unsettling experience ... something about entering an airtight container where the oxygen was regulated by a reference librarian.
~ *Dan Brown (Angels and Demons. Simon & Schuster, 2000, p. 193.)*

Most people don't realize how important librarians are. I ran across a book recently which suggested that the peace and prosperity of a culture was solely related to how many librarians it contained. Possibly a slight overstatement. But a culture that doesn't value its librarians doesn't value ideas and without ideas, well, where are we?
~ *Neil Gaiman (The Sandman)*

To Homer, libraries were holy places like churches, and the priestly librarians a blessed race, a saving remnant in a world of sin. Whenever God grew impatient and decided to destroy the world he remembered the librarians and stayed his hand.
~ *Jane Langton (The Thief of Venice, February 2001)*

# On Bookstores

Where is human nature so weak as in the bookstore?
~ *Henry Ward Beecher*

The smallest bookstore still contains more ideas of worth than have been presented in the entire history of television."
~ *Andrew Ross*

Also, if nothing else, writing this book has really changed the way I experience bookstores. I have a whole different appreciation for the amount of work packed into even the slimmest volume on the shelves.
~ *Jesse James Garrett*

Bookstores see a book by a woman and they put it in the romance section.
~ *Barbara Taylor Bradford*

Don't patronize the chain bookstores. Every time I see some author scheduled to read and sign his books at a chain bookstore, I feel like telling him he's stabbing the independent bookstores in the back.
~ *Lawrence Ferlinghetti*

The more I do bookstores, the more people come up to me from church groups. I spoke at Pittsburg State College and had 2 or 3 ministers and book groups from a couple of churches.
~ *Anita Diament*

There's nothing definite yet. Of course, any time you have a book, there's going to be book signings and stuff. We'll do bookstores that handle both audio and video. And some of the stores want to have the CDs available at the same time. So that part looks real good.
~ *Scotty Moore*

We're competing with everything: the beach, the mall, bookstores. Libraries are in a transition right now, caught between two forces, the old ways and technology. Libraries are under a lot of pressure to provide both.
~ *John Callahan*

I went to a bookstore and asked the saleswoman, Where's the self-help section? She said if she told me, it would defeat the purpose.
~ *George Carlin (American stand-up Comedian, Actor and Author. b.1937)*

A man in a bookstore buys a book on loneliness and every woman in the store hits on him. A woman buys a book on loneliness and the store clears out.
~ *Doug Coupland*

By then I was in Brooklyn and drank my way through that summer. I stopped when I got sick of that and got a job at the Strand bookstore, which was a little better than the tax job.
~ *Robert Quine*

Genre is a bookstore problem, not a literary problem.
~ *Rick Moody*

The book salesman should be honored because he brings to our attention, as a rule, the very books we need most and neglect most.
~ *Frank Crane*

Here, you can walk into a bookstore and pick up a Bible or Christian literature and learn. Over there, they are lucky if they have one Bible for a whole village.
~ *Michael Scott*

I can walk into a bookstore and hand over my credit card and they don't know who the hell I am. Maybe that says something about bookstore clerks.
~ *E. L. Doctorow*

I was in Paris at an English-language bookstore. I picked up a volume of Dickinson's poetry. I came back to my hotel, read 2,000 of her poems and immediately began composing in my head. I wrote down the melodies even before I got to a piano.
~ *Gordon Getty*

I get crazy in a bookstore. It makes my heart beat hard because I want to buy everything.
~ *Reese Witherspoon*

A bookstore is one of the only pieces of evidence we have that people are still thinking.
~ *Jerry Seinfeld*

I work full-time in a used bookstore. I get up. I drink a cup of coffee. I think, The last thing I want to do is write. Then I go to the computer and write.
~ *Kate DiCamillo*

I'm totally into new age and self-help books. I used to work in a bookstore and that's the section they gave me, and I got way into it. I just loved the power of positive thinking, letting yourself go.
~ *Jason Mraz*

It's one thing for the people in the industry to know who you are, because they've heard about you earlier. I have friends calling me from the Christian bookstore because there's a poster on the wall. It's just weird.
~ *Stacie Orrico*

My goal is two pages a day, five days a week. I never want to write, but I'm always glad that I have done it. After I write, I go to work at the bookstore.
~ *Kate DiCamillo*

We were just a one-room bookstore; we didn't have any money for lawyers.
~ *Lawrence Ferlinghetti*

If Jack Kerouac had set out to find a real bookstore in the suburbs, he would still be on the road, Phileas Fogg would still be in the air, the Ancient Mariner wouldn't have had time to tell anyone his story.
~ *Michael Winerip*

The independent bookstore-you know we're almost dinosaurs.
~ *Carl A. Kroch*

The independent bookstores that are left have learned how to compete in this marketplace. There are fewer bookstores now, but the ones that are left are not only a good place to buy books, but they are also well-run businesses."
~ *Hut Landon*

Out of the closets and into the museums, libraries, architectural monuments, concert halls, bookstores, recording studios and film studios of the world. Everything belongs to the inspired and dedicated thief... Words, colors, light, sounds, stone, wood, bronze belong to the living artist. They belong to anyone who can use them. Loot the Louver! A bas l Originality, the sterile and assertive ego that imprisons us as it creates. Vive le sol ~ pure, shameless, total. We are not responsible. Steal anything in sight.
~ *William S. Burroughs*

In spite of the six thousand manuals on child raising in the bookstores, child raising is still a dark continent and no one really knows anything. You just need a lot of love and luck ~ and, of course, courage.
~ *Bill Cosby*

This is a feminist bookstore. There is no humor section.
~ *John Callahan*

# Name Index

## A

Abraham Lincoln, 55, 98, 131, 159, 175, 194
Adrienne Yorinks, 250
Agnes George DeMille, 79, 204, 261
Aimee Mann, 84, 175
Alan Paton, 111
Albert Camus, 21
Albert Einstein, 153
Alberto Manguel, 72, 175
Aldous Huxley, 52, 68, 111, 195
Aleksandr Isayevich Solzhenitsyn, 195
Alexander Graham Bell, 196, 242
Alexander Pope, 196
Alexander Smith, 135, 214, 217, 246
Alex Haley, 206
Alfred Hitchcock, 153
Alfred Jarry, 193
Alfred Kazin, 251
Alice Hoffman, 105
Allan Bloom, 38, 72
Ambrose Bierce, 99, 191
American Proverb, 31, 98
Amos Bronson Alcott, 36, 164, 196, 234
Amy Lowell, 29, 106, 125–26, 135, 140
Anatole France, 48, 116, 134
Andre Gide, 175
Andre Maurois, 138, 199
Andre Sinyavsky, 33
Andrew Carnegie, 233
Andrew Lang, 154
Andy Gates, 82
Aneurin Bevan, 20
Angela Carter, 176
Anita Brookner, 39
Anita Diament, 262
Anna Garlin Spencer, 156
Anna Green, 190
Anna Karenina, 95

Anna Quindlen, 86–87, 139, 154
Anne Fine, 85
Anne Frank, 135
Anne Rice, 176
Ann Richards, 126
Anthony Burgess, 40
Anthony Hope, 26
Anthony Marcel, 70, 172
Anthony Powell, 136
Anthony Trollope, 176
Anton Chekhov, 189
Anu Garg, 103
Archibald Macleish, 196, 213, 235, 252
Arnold Bennett, 38
Arnold Lobel, 154
Arthur Ashe, 208, 225
Arthur C. Clarke, 183
Arthur Christopher Benson, 20, 176
Arthur James Balfour, 183
Arthur Meier Schlesinger, 234
Arthur Miller, 191
Arthur Schopenhauer, 33, 61–62, 112, 207
Ashleigh Brilliant, 208
A. S. W. Rosenbach, 32
Augustine Birrell, 117, 163, 173, 219, 238
Augustus Hare, 94, 164

## B

Barbara Kingsolver, 257
Barbara Taylor Bradford, 262
Barbara W. Tuchman, 79, 81, 95, 104, 133, 139, 207, 212, 218
Benjamin Disraeli, 44–45, 108
Benjamin Franklin, 25, 105, 150, 182–83, 190
Benjamin Jowett, 53
Bernard Keble Sandwell, 232
Bernie Hubley, 81
Bertrand Russell, 72
Bert Williams, 36
Bette Midler, 113

# Subject Index